WHERE

GOD

LIVES

WHERE GOD LIVES

THE SCIENCE OF THE PARANORMAL AND HOW OUR BRAINS ARE LINKED TO THE UNIVERSE

MELVIN MORSE, M.D.
with Paul Perry

HarperOne
An Imprint of HarperCollinsPublishers

HarperOne

HarperCollins books may be purchased for educational,
business, or sales promotional use. For information
please write: Special Markets Department, HarperCollins
Publishers, 10 East 53rd Street, New York, NY 10022.

HarperCollins Web site: http://www.harpercollins.com

HarperCollins®, 🔲 ®, and HarperOne™ are trademarks
of HarperCollins Publishers.

FIRST CLIFF STREET BOOKS PAPERBACK EDITION
PUBLISHED IN 2001

Library of Congress Cataloging-in-Publication Data is
available upon request.

ISBN 978–0–06–109504–7

10 11 12 RRD(H) 10 9 8

CONTENTS

CONTENTS

ACKNOWLEDGMENTS

THIS BOOK IS DEDICATED TO MY OFFICE NURSE, TRISH. THE essential questions of the book were framed during dozens of hours of discussions primarily at Mariners baseball games. She provided invaluable insights into the Christian religious tradition and served as the religious counterpoint to my scientific attempts to understand the nature of God. She helped me understand the religious consequences of my theories.

I also want to thank our nutritionist, Joanne Montzingo. She encouraged me to run and was kind enough to slow her pace to encourage a plodder such as myself. She taught me the importance of doing three sets of fifteen jumping jacks as a most excellent spiritual and physical warm-up for any athletic event. Her own life is proof of my theories.

Paul Perry took the seven or eight hundred chaotic, disorganized, rambling pages of material I sent him and turned it into the fine-tuned machine that this book is. I am probably the only person who truly understands his genius in taking complex scientific concepts and making them seem simple. This is the fourth book we have written together and far and away our best.

I thank my editor, Diane Reverand, for her patience and faith in this book and, by extension, in my theories and me.

I thank my agent, Nat Sobel, for patience above and beyond the call of duty. This book would not have happened without him.

I particularly want to thank Robert Bigelow and the scientists at the National Institute of Discovery Science. Being a member of the nation's top consciousness-studies think tank gave me access to the top theoretical physicists, astrophysicists, cosmologists, molecular biologists, and consciousness thinkers in the country. Much of the material in this book was developed in van rides to and from the meetings of the institute.

I especially want to thank Colm Kelleher, John and Victoria Alexender, and Alina Caro.

My front office staff has patiently had to put up with hundreds of phone calls about my research, which have nothing to do with my full-time practice of medicine. I want to thank Tiki for extraordinary fax machine and scheduling abilities. Jolene Meade runs my website and keeps me organized.

My income is from my private practice of medicine. I do not have the pressures of conforming to tenure committees and the irrational skepticism often seen in the academic world, as my patients provide me with my income. Any contributions I have made toward understanding human consciousness have come about because my patients trust me with the care of their children. I am first and foremost a pediatrician.

I could not have written this book without the support of my family: my wife, Allison, and my children, Bridget, Colleen, Brett, Cody, and Michaela.

My mother, Gertrude Morse, started my interest in near death studies by introducing me to Bruce Greyson, the acknowledged father of near death research. Bruce has been my mentor and my inspiration.

Finally, I want to thank the children who contributed to my research and studies. They are the source of my inspiration. I am honored that they have been able to share their stories with me. The near death picnic in this book was based on a series of picnics held yearly at my horse farm in Maple Valley, Washington. This book was directly inspired by those meetings with remarkable young men and women.

Simple Prayers, Complex Results

> A miracle is not the breaking of laws, nor is it a phenomenon outside of laws. It is laws that are incomprehensible and unknown to us, and are therefore miraculous.
>
> —*Gurdjieff*

IN 1997, NEUROSCIENTISTS FROM THE UNIVERSITY OF CALIFORnia at San Diego bravely proclaimed that they had found an area of the human brain that "may be hardwired to hear the voice of heaven." In specially designed research, they found that certain parts of the brain—the right temporal lobe, to be exact—were attuned to ideas about the supreme being and mystical experiences. They called this area "the God Module" and said it was "dedicated machinery for religion."

Many scientists were excited by the research. One, Craig Kinsley, a neuroscientist at the University of Richmond, in Virginia, even declared, "There is a quandary of whether the mind created God or God created the mind. This is going to shake people up."

I knew what he meant. In three other books, I had already identified the right temporal lobe as the place where man interfaces with God. It is this area, an area I call "the God Spot," that is an area of untapped and unlimited potential where God lives in each of us. This region is instrumental in facilitating mind-body healing. It is responsible for visions as well as psychic powers and vivid spiritual experiences.

In short, the right temporal lobe allows us to interact actively with the universe.

Although the events of a near death experience, or NDE, represent what is thought to be our final communication and interaction with the universe, that couldn't be further from the truth. NDEs are simply spiritual experiences that occur while we are dying. What we learn from studying NDEs is that we have the biological potential to interact with the universe at any time during our lives. In order to do so, we just have to learn how to activate the right temporal lobe, the place where God lives.

As a practicing pediatrician with an interest in near death studies, I have seen what happens when this area is activated in children who have had NDEs. I have also seen how these children are affected in the years following their brush with death. Not only are these children better balanced in their physical and mental lives, but they are better balanced spiritually. They eat better food, do better in school, and are more mature than most of their peers. They are aware of a connection with the universe that most other kids don't even know exists. They feel a purpose in living, and they don't fear that death is the "end of it all." They trust their intuitions and feel they can connect again with the divine presence they saw when they nearly died, *without having nearly to die again.*

"Once you've seen the light on the other side, you can see it again if you try," said one of my young patients. "It is always there for you."

WHERE IS IT?

Don't look for the God Spot in an anatomy book. Modern medical science does not officially recognize this area of the brain, or any other area, for that matter, as the God Spot. In fact, standard textbooks of neurology describe the function of the right temporal lobe as that of processing and interpreting memories and emotions. In *Where God Lives*, the right temporal lobe will be shown to function as a "paranormal" area, which gives us such abilities as mind-body healing, telepathy, and the ability to communicate with God. Since these abilities are paranormal, they are controversial. So it naturally follows that there is no official medical recognition of the God Spot or anything else like it.

How could this be? How could we, for thousands of years, ignore something as important as the ability to interact with God? The simple answer would be that we are in the "spiritual dark ages" and have yet to evolve out of them. The history of humankind is filled with such intellectual blind spots. The Chinese invented the compass, but not for travel. Rather, they used this amazing instrument to align their homes geographically, for mystical reasons. The Mayans invented the wheel, but used it only for children's toys. It wasn't for many years that other cultures discovered additional uses for these inventions and used them to change the course of history. It will be a long time before Western medicine acknowledges an area of the brain that interacts with the universe, despite research by respectable institutions. Even though doctors act on intuition with this area of the brain every day in their medical practices, most deal with the "mind-body connection" as a concept rather than a reality. An actual God Spot? No way.

I WAS ONE OF THEM

Of course, I understand why most Western-trained medical doctors don't acknowledge the God Spot as an anatomical area. After all, I went to medical school at Johns Hopkins University, one of America's bastions of medical education. Had one of us even considered proposing something so nebulous and out of the mainstream as an area of the brain that interacts with God, we would not have been taken seriously.

My strict medical training led me to deny the existence of such an amazing area of the brain. Even when I started studying near death experiences and focused on interviewing hundreds of children who had nearly died, I had trouble believing everything I was hearing. I interviewed children who had left their dead bodies on emergency room tables and "floated" to the waiting room to visit with their concerned families. Later, they were able to recall conversations and scenes that they could not possibly have witnessed in their comatose state.

Still, I had trouble accepting the reality of the near death experience, largely because my strict scientific training made me suspicious of unexplained events. I was like a man who reads books about surviving in the wilderness but has never actually camped out at night to put those skills to work.

Then, one day, I saw the light. I was speaking to a group of electroencephalographers, people who use EEG machines, when one of the technicians asked, "How can you stimulate your right temporal lobe?"

I responded technically, telling her about a neurologist who used electricity to stimulate the right temporal lobe artificially. In the middle of my response she impatiently interrupted, "No, I mean how can you do it naturally?"

I shrugged and said the first thing that came into my mind. "I guess that's what people do when they pray."

TASTE OF MY OWN MEDICINE

I never thought to try this time-tested method of right-temporal-lobe stimulation, this thing called "prayer," myself. I was like most doctors who rarely taste the medicine they dispense. I kept it at a distance, using it to explain my work but never praying in my own life. I can honestly say that I had never truly prayed until I was forty years old.

Almost on a dare, I decided to take a leap of faith. My leap happened during the publicity tour for our third book, *Parting Visions*. Book tours are fast-paced events in which authors often run from interview to interview. The relentless pace is monitored by a media escort who specializes in getting authors from one interview to the next. It is a mind-numbing exercise, answering the same questions over and over again, trying to summarize such a complex topic as spiritual visions into three or six minutes or whatever time bite before the next commercial break. Book tours are tough duty, but they have value beyond just selling books. For one thing, they give me an opportunity to learn firsthand how people feel about my research.

One of these opportunities came in the Midwest, where I was picked up at the airport by a media escort whose husband had recently died of cancer. It was one of those days during which nothing seems to go right. Several radio stations canceled their interviews with me, and I was left to do nothing but kill time with my media escort.

She was deeply religious and had no doubt whatsoever that there was life after death. Her terminally ill husband had true spiritual visions of another life, she said, and she saw his visions as an affirmation of her lifelong faith. She treasured, rather than feared, his final moments of life.

"How do we connect to God?" she asked.

I told her my theory of the God Spot, and how I now realized that it could be "turned on" in a number of ways besides near death or actually dying. I mentioned a number of studies in which the right temporal lobe had been stimulated and spiritual experiences "turned on" as a result. I also mentioned that "true prayer" could turn it on. "But," I said, "I am not sure what 'true prayer' really is."

"You must know what it is," she said. "You have never prayed?"

I had to answer, honestly, that I had not. I prayed when my dad had cancer, but I felt that it was just a way of expressing extreme anxiety. Even though I attended Hebrew school as a child, the prayers we said there seemed to be the meaningless chanting of ancient writings.

I had no trouble with the pursuit of science as a sort of religion. Although much of my work had involved leaps of faith, they were calculated leaps backed up by scientific research that made them very short and safe. But religion, I told this woman, was on the other side of a gap that was too wide for me to cross.

"Perhaps," she said. "But I didn't ask you if you were religious. I asked if you have ever prayed. Don't you think prayer and religion can be two different things?"

I had never thought of them separately, I said, but I saw how prayer and religion could be used together or separately as the gateway to spirituality. I also mentioned that religion is frequently used as a method of control rather than a means of freeing one's soul.

"Don't think about all of the bad that has happened as a result of religion," she said. "Just think about the creator of the universe and about trying to touch that power. Just get on your knees and talk to God. If you do it right, maybe God will respond."

I laughed, then said, "Well, maybe I will try it."

"Promise me that you'll try it tonight."

"Okay," I promised. "I'll try it tonight."

PROMISE KEPT, QUESTION ASKED

Later that night, as promised, I knelt at the foot of my bed. It didn't feel as dumb as I thought it would. I thought lovingly about each of my children, laughed about something each of them had said, and thanked God for them. I thought of my wife and how lucky I was to have someone who could put up with my devotion to the practice of medicine. I prayed for the health of my patients and that I would have the insight to help them. And then I decided to ask God a question. I asked, "What is the nature of God, and what is the relationship between God and man?"

I know my prayer seemed contrived, but I was acting with a completely open heart. In the end, I sincerely and openly prayed for about five minutes that night. I followed the formula my escort had outlined for me, a few minutes thanking God for my blessings, a few minutes praying for others, and then my question.

To make my experiment with prayer more scientific, I included in my prayer that I had to have the answer within a twenty-four-hour period. That way there would be a clear end point, and I wouldn't have to wonder if events during the next several days could be interpreted as God's answer to my question.

The next day I got up early and flew to Los Angeles, where I faced a busy schedule of radio and TV appearances. By midafternoon I had completely forgotten about my prayer experiment. When I got to the hotel that evening, exhausted, I got my answer. Filled with pent-up energy, and pacing around my hotel room, I was suddenly surrounded by an incredible light that gave me a sense of peace, calm, and love.

I knew what it was immediately. The slight hiss I had been hearing in my ear all day from clenching my jaw muscles was gone. In fact, all sound was gone. I felt immersed in a sweet, warm, honeylike feeling. I could feel it on my skin as much as feel it in my heart and brain.

I felt completely at peace, surrounded by love. I knew everything. I suddenly felt that if I asked any question, I would immediately know the answer. I heard my question again, in my head, "What is the nature of God, and what is the relationship between God and man?"

I understood that man and everything else in the universe is a piece of God. As each snowflake contains miniature representations of the entire snowflake, and each strand of human DNA contains the code to create a unique human, we are all tiny pieces of God.

The sensation of being exposed to this universal light was like doing a belly flop off the high dive. All the wind was knocked out of me. My entire body experienced an intense pain and then all feelings and sensations ceased. In one blinding flash, I suddenly understood I was a body within a soul, not the other way around.

I understood this all in an instant, an instant that seemed to be never ending. I had studied this sort of experience for years in other people, but never until then did I have one myself.

Such an epiphany has not yet been repeated, even though I have prayed many times since. It was enough to have had it happen once, because now I know I can communicate with God in times of need, a belief of virtually every religion. I am confident that this experience will be there for me again if I ever really need it.

THE BOTTOM LINE

My work with children who have had NDEs and my own spiritual experience have taught me some valuable lessons that I may not always follow but that are always present in my mind: My wife and children are the most important gifts in my life, love is the fabric that binds humanity together, and few things are really worth getting "worked up" over.

I don't want to portray myself as a minor saint. I still yell at my kids at the end of a long weekend when everyone is tired. I still can be insensitive, stare at the TV too much, and not listen to my wife attentively. I still can be grouchy at work. But I realize that all of life is brief and precious. "We only have a few minutes," Billy Graham has said. "The great mystery of life is how short it is."

My brief right-temporal-lobe awakening has led me to have confidence in the rest of my right-temporal-lobe abilities—telepathy, remote viewing, and mind-body healing. I have learned to trust my instincts and to see intuition as an asset that is biologically hardwired in our brains.

After fifteen years of listening to children describing what it was like when they died, I have learned that what happened to them in what were almost their final moments of life can happen to any of us, at any time throughout our lives. The experiences teach us that we have a large area of the brain—our right temporal lobe—that remains underused. It is now a scientific fact—which I will establish in this book—that when this area functions fully, we receive insight into the meaning of life and a personal introduction to God.

For most of us, the search for spirituality is like the man who searched for fire with a lighted candle. Fire was in front of his face all of the time, he was just looking beyond it.

We often ignore the insights and visions we obtain from our right temporal lobe. We don't trust them, or we don't believe the answer to our problems could be so simple.

As you will discover in this book, the right temporal lobe is giving us insights about living all the time. The challenge is to learn how to hear that inner voice, and distinguish between the insight presented to us by the right temporal lobe and the cacophony of other voices and feelings that clutter our brain. This reminds me of a story a child once told me when she recounted the particulars of her near death experience. She said she went to a "place of light" where she encountered a frantic little man who was a picture of frustration. When she asked him what was wrong, he told her, "They keep praying to me for answers, and I keep sending them answers, but they never seem to listen or hear."

LEARNING TO LISTEN

Learning how to listen to our inner voice is what this book is all about. It is a voice we all know exists. That inner guidance system tells us who we are and where we are going. It is our connection with the divine. It is the divine light seen by many who have had NDEs. As one child who nearly died of bacterial meningitis described it, "It's the light that told me who I was and where I was to go."

Of course, none of us should wait until we die to learn who we are and where we are to go. We urgently need to connect with that light right now. And you can. By reading this book, you will discover that this spiritual light is available to you throughout the rest of your life. It is easier to experience than you think. You just have to want it.

1

The Near Death Picnic

IT WAS GOOD TO SEE THE KIDS AGAIN, THE ONES WHO WERE the subjects of my initial research into the occurrence of near death experiences (NDEs) in children. Their stories were first told seven years ago in *Closer to the Light* and fifteen years after my encounter with Katie, the young lady whose remarkable story launched me on this path of exploration. Seeing them again, I couldn't believe how much they'd grown and changed, but that's how it is with kids, isn't it?

They had been arriving all afternoon with their families to visit with my wife and me. We had the perfect place for a picnic—plenty of open space for games, horses to ride, a pond, barns to explore, and fields to walk in. This was one of many such picnics we'd had for these children who'd crossed the threshold of death and lived to tell their miraculous stories. These picnics were an opportunity to catch up and have a good time but, more important, they were a chance to learn how the NDEs they'd had as small children influenced who they were today.

Judging from everything I'd seen and heard so far, their lives were unfolding in remarkable ways. As a group, these young people were different from their peers. Different, not just because they nearly died when they were young, but because of the unique perceptions and outlooks that their NDEs had brought to them.

The commonly perceived boundaries of personal growth and potential seem to be irrelevant to them. They possess intuitive and empathetic natures that put them in touch with aspects of our world about which most of us only dream. Their NDEs have given them a variety of unusual abilities, like telepathy or the power to perceive the future.

They also stand out for other, more obvious reasons. They're a solid, steady group. In growing up, they've managed to avoid many of the pitfalls in judgment that have ensnared others their age. Not one of the girls in this group of thirty is pregnant, nor is anyone addicted to drugs or alcohol. All are achievers in their own way.

There's a lesson we can all learn from these children, one which those of us who haven't had an NDE can appreciate. It is a lesson of mystical unity with the universe. These children have often expressed to me such ideas as "I learned that we are all connected," "I learned that everything is important," "I see pieces of that light everywhere." These children describe precisely the same insights as those of the mystics who are present in virtually every society throughout human history.

This awareness is encouraging. Not only do they tell me that mystical experiences transform people, but they represent a change in thinking, a paradigm shift, about the end of life and its implications.

Scientist and author James Burke has detailed many of these paradigm shifts in human consciousness over thousands of years. He points out that the changes occur through the process of new data being discovered that are not explainable under the old world view of what is real.

These new facts, often discovered by chance or serendipity, lead to a tension in which the old order is vigorously defended by a dying generation of scientists and philosophers even as new ideas emerge. Change is never easy and is rarely welcomed by those who are comfortable with the familiar and are in positions of power.

THE SCIENCE OF CHANGE

Those in the field of science are no exception to these prejudices. Even so, change is part of the important process of scientific progress. Take the Viennese obstetrician Ignaz Philipp Semmelweis. In 1861, he showed conclusively that women were dying of childbirth fever because physicians didn't wash their hands between autopsies and deliveries. In the absence of a "germ theory," they saw no reason to. Semmelweis's ideas about the existence of invisible agents of disease were laughable to right-thinking scientists of the day.

It took fifty years for hand-washing to catch on. It took the invention of the microscope, Lister's invention of the germ theory, and, finally, a younger generation of scientists before hand-washing became standard procedure. This younger generation was able to see clinical data objectively—women who were attended to by physicians who washed their hands had better outcomes than those with doctors who didn't wash their hands. A change in clinical practice followed.

A more recent example of a discovery changing medicine is the finding in the early nineties that a common bacteria caused most cases of ulcers, and not high levels of stress, as was thought for so many years. This discovery, not widely accepted in the beginning by most doctors, has completely changed the treatment of ulcers. Now most cases of ulcers are treated rapidly and successfully with antibiotics instead of with surgery, antacids, and changes in diet that do not work.

The bottom line is that a paradigm shift occurs only when the old theory cannot explain new scientific data. And yet, new facts can only be understood and accepted once there is a scientific theory and framework in which to place them.

In the 1700s, French peasants reported strange sightings—rocks that came from the sky. Even though their accounts of this phenomenon were well documented, it wasn't until scientific theory progressed enough to understand planetary motion around the sun, and gravity, that scientists accepted that meteors were real.

The same is true of reports of ball lightning. Such sightings were similarly dismissed as hallucinations or mass hysteria despite astute observations by such reliable sources as airline pilots. Not until theoretical physics progressed to explain the phenomenon did it receive acceptance among the general scientific community.

The same is true with the NDE studies I conducted at Children's Hospital in Seattle. I collected information from children who nearly died and who shared with me their observations and encounters at the point of death. Their experiences have many common denominators—a sense of leaving their physical bodies, having contact with a consciousness even though their physical bodies were clinically dead, and encountering an all-knowing, loving being that most of the children call God. They also experienced the sensation of bright light and recall encounters and conversations with dead relatives.

The experience, itself, transcends what we consider to be ordinary time; in fact, it seems timeless. When they return to the reality we all share, they have new information and abilities. Some have even gone on to become millionaires because of inventions and patents they developed from information they obtained in this timeless, all-knowing state.

Some invest their unique gifts in helping others understand that death isn't something to fear, but is rather a holy experience to be embraced, when the time is right.

One of my study participants at the near death picnic was sharing her gift for drawing by doing face-painting for the littlest kids.

As a young girl, she drew hundreds of pictures of her NDE, often using different materials or colors, and yet drawing the same scene again and again. At the bottom of the drawing, she is being examined by doctors, including my partner, David Christopher. The drawing is so accurate in its detail it could come from a textbook on cardiac resuscitation, right down to the location of his hands on her chest. She then shows herself floating out of her body, meeting Jesus and angels, and seeing a light that told her "who I was and where I was to go."

Ten years later, she has little to say about the experience, but her fascination with drawing attests to its power in her life. She often takes her work to hospitals and shows it to children who are dying. "It's something I can give back," she explains. "It helps the kids and their parents understand the experience that's ahead. I think it lessens their fear and gives them some hope."

Although she doesn't speak of it herself, I've heard from others that she possesses a real and unexplained ability to help children cope with the pain of dying. She, like others in my study, seems to have an inherent understanding of the link between the mind and the body.

REACHING THROUGH TIME AND SPACE

At the near death picnic I was joined by Katie, who jumped down from the corral fence and came over to stand beside me. "This is great. I can't believe everyone's here," she said. "You know, I've been thinking about you a lot lately and remembering the first time we talked. Do you remember?"

How could I forget? I first met Katie fifteen years ago when she was nine. She'd been found floating facedown in a swimming pool, and no one knew how long she'd been unconscious. I was doing my internship in pediatrics in a small town in Idaho when I helped resuscitate her. At the time, she was one of the sickest children I had ever cared for. I was sure she was going to die.

But she didn't. Instead, she made a full recovery, and at her follow-up visit, I remember marveling at her. Her eyes revealed an intelligence that hadn't been dimmed by the deprivation of oxygen to the brain that often accompanies drowning. Even though she was unconscious in the emergency room, she recalled in vivid detail the treatment she received and the people who administered it. When I asked her what she remembered about being in the swimming pool, she said, "Do you mean when I visited with the Heavenly Father and Jesus?"

That response, along with other recollections Katie shared with me on subsequent visits, forever changed my way of thinking about illness and death.

Katie recounted moving through a tunnel and being met by a brightly lit figure, of visiting her home and seeing her parents engaged in everyday activities that turned out to have actually occurred while she was unconscious. She made friends in this sort of afterworld and clearly enjoyed her stay. And then she returned to her family to grow to be the lovely young woman standing beside me.

"Of course I remember the first time we met," I said. "How much of it do you remember?"

"Oh, I remember everything, every little detail, and they're images that are always with me," she confided. "My life is richer for it and I work every day to share that richness with my family and friends. There's so much work to do in this life. I wouldn't waste a minute of it." Katie's attitude is typical of these young people. She was transformed by her experience and demonstrates this transformation in her ability to sense energy fields in others.

Many of the children from my study have the innate ability to reach easily and naturally through the commonly accepted boundaries of time and matter. Some have reported seeing and conversing with apparitions—ghosts or angels, if you will.

Others, like Darren, continue to have what I call prelife visions. When he was six, he was diagnosed with a neuroblastoma, a kind of cancer, and given a grim prognosis. But Darren wasn't having any of it. He had a vision in which his tumor disappeared and even drew a picture of himself without the tumor. Since that day, he's been in remission.

Today, he's a natural comic, at ease with little kids as well as with adults. He uses his gift to guide others, to provide insight and support. No one in attendance at our picnic would have ever suspected that the young man who was loading my flatbed with hay in preparation for the afternoon's hay ride was studying for the priesthood and hopes one day to devote himself to work in hospices.

The same spiritual devotion was present in Andrew, another of my NDE patients who was sharing barbecue duty with me. Amid the hot coals and smoke, he was telling me about his work as a physical therapist and Little League coach. He was pursuing these "helping activities," he said, because of the NDE he had experienced as a very young infant.

"You know, when we talked about what I remember when I almost died, I thought it was the most ordinary thing in the world. But I was just a baby when it happened. I didn't know any better. I didn't realize that it was something that was going to guide me throughout my life," he said.

Andrew's experience was unique in that he was just nine months old when his NDE occurred. He'd had cardiac arrest and found himself floating above his body. He then flew into the waiting room where he could see his grandparents crying. He crawled up a long, dark tunnel with the aid of an unseen hand. When he reached his destination, he ran through fields with God. His memory of this event has faded, but not the conviction that he has important work to do in this life.

"That experience rewired me and made me different from everyone else," he declared. "From as early as I can remember, I have had a purpose in life. I am guided by that light and what it showed me."

These children came from all backgrounds in life, rich and poor, with various ethnicities and different religious upbringings. One boy who opened his eyes immediately after having cardiac arrest fifteen years ago looked directly at me and said, "Dr. Morse, I have a wonderful secret to tell you. I have been climbing a staircase to heaven." Though he has no memory of that today, he has grown to be an energetic young man whose intuition and creativity set him apart from his peers at college. He's forgotten the staircase to heaven, but he clearly is capable of climbing to great heights.

Those who do remember tell me it was an experience with a clear meaning. One little girl said, "I learned that life is for living, and that the light will always be with me." That's the kind of life-changing insight for which many people wait their whole lives. Today, that young lady is an empathetic listener and natural problem solver. She helped to organize a softball game for the younger children and was more than willing to take the catcher's position so she could give encouragement to the opposing team's hitters.

Everyone in the NDE debate agrees that the experience itself is vividly real. It has the unmistakable, ineffable quality of reality. For many of those who have had the experience, there is no debate—*res ipsa loquitur*—the thing speaks for itself.

Even so, as these children have grown to be young men and women, they've begun questioning their memories and have come to me asking, "Was it real?" It's a thought-provoking inquiry, because the proof lies just outside our conscious grasp. Perhaps the answer lies closer to a comment from Dr. William Wommack, one of my most severe critics at Seattle Children's Hospital, who nonetheless said, "It isn't the experience that is or isn't real. It is the transformation that is real."

As I watched Marla play shortstop, I remembered her case. She was part of my study because she had survived a coma with a Glasgow coma score of three, a level normally associated with certain death. She has no memory of almost drowning, but her father does.

He and a friend dived repeatedly into the lake to rescue her. The sky was overcast and the water so murky he couldn't see anything. On their final dive, they saw her. She was illuminated by an inner light that guided them to her. That inner light still shines brightly today.

Bob, her father, and I sat together watching the softball action in the shade of a towering maple. "Move up on it, move up on it," Jim shouted to Marla, who nabbed a fast-moving grounder and fired it to first base. "That girl can play. She's not like any other teenager I know. She's got drive and ambition, but it's not mean-spirited. Did I tell you she's tutoring little kids in reading?" It doesn't surprise me one bit.

HARDWIRED FOR LIFE

Many more questions than answers remain about NDEs. What we do know is that the seat of NDEs, the place in the human brain in which they are manifest, is the right temporal lobe.

Little about the brain can be neatly localized to one particular area. The brain is so flexible and amazing that it duplicates its abilities in many different areas. Memories and abilities thought to reside in, say, the left half of the brain, where our speech abilities lie, may also exist in the right half. When I say that heaven and God can be perceived through our right temporal lobes, I really mean to include other associated deep structures that are closely allied with the right temporal lobe. Specifically, these include the hippocampus and other closely related limbic lobe structures, all of which have a role in controlling memory and emotions.

One hundred years ago, researchers began to map the functions of various parts of the brain. This research demonstrated that our right temporal lobe, in addition to aiding in hearing, smelling, and taste, is also capable of mystical perceptions of God and other spiritual reality, most notably the ability to perceive this reality from a point of view outside the body, or to have the so-called out-of-body experience.

By the end of the nineteenth century, anatomists observed that patients who had brain tumors or other lesions in the right temporal lobe had complex visual hallucinations of people and events, projected three dimensionally outside their bodies. A seizure in the right temporal lobe might lead someone to see the face of God repeatedly or to have out-of-body experiences.

Nearly forty years ago, Wilder Penfield, then the preeminent authority on neurosurgery, discovered that electrical stimulation applied to a specific area of the right temporal lobe brought about NDE-like sensations—people hearing beautiful music, seeing dead friends and relatives, as well as having a life review. This area—the Sylvian fissure—is in the right temporal lobe, just above the ear.

Penfield took long stainless steel needles and shocked areas within the brain in conscious patients who were undergoing neurosurgery. He found that when he stimulated areas in the right temporal lobe, patients reported having out-of-body experiences, seeing lights and geometrical shapes, viewing memories from their lives replayed in three-dimensional form outside their bodies, and virtually every other element attributed to the NDE. Penfield reported, for example, one patient stating, "Oh God, I'm leaving my body," and, even more interesting, "I'm half in and half out."

Similarly, Canadian consciousness researcher Michael Persinger has documented that stimulating the right temporal lobe with electricity appears to bring about the beneficial effects of what he calls "the God experience." He goes so far as to recommend the induction of this experience through meditation or prayer for all human beings as an antidote to the violence, depression, drug addiction, and collapse of social structures that currently plague our society.

Dr. Persinger feels his research shows that the perception of God, including its transformative effects, can be duplicated by electrical-stimulation studies similar to the ones he did. He states, "The capacity to have the God experience is a consequence of the human brain's construction. If the temporal lobe had developed in some other way, the God experience would not have occurred."

He further makes this telling observation: Most of us have learned to compartmentalize the God experience. It can be conditioned to occur only at certain times or in certain places. Because of the relationship between the frontal lobes (those involved in decision making) and the temporal lobes (those having to do with memory, the interpretation of experience, and the God experience), most of us can learn to control the experience of perceiving God.

But why does the experience occur at all? Some people think it's a primitive defense mechanism, one that, when an individual is at the point of death, serves to comfort him. Others believe it encourages kinship loyalty or stability within an interdependent group, for example, a tribe or a family.

This does not imply that faith is purely a matter of brain physiology and chemistry. Rather, it may merely document which region of the brain is most involved in faith.

The other functions of the right temporal lobe permit the perception of memories and the interpretation of experience. This allows the transforming aspects of the God experience to be generalized to the entire personality. Related areas of the brain also permit the experience of light. When the entire circuit works correctly, the person having the experience of a properly functioning right temporal lobe perceives a mystical light, and identifies it as God. This, in turn, has a profound transforming effect on the individual's personality.

Certainly, I am not the first to make this connection. Many others have seen it before. Philosopher and neuroscientist Arthur Mandell states that the "kingdom of heaven can be found in the right temporal lobe." Most scientists have denied it. A few, frightened by the implications, have pushed it into the corners of scientific study. There it has stayed, pigeonholed, as an abnormal mental event.

EXPLORING THE UNKNOWN

The history of science is closely tied to what a society is capable of believing. Let's examine the simultaneous and independent invention of the mathematical principles of calculus by Sir Isaac Newton and the great Japanese mathematician Takakazu Seki.

In Newton's day, the belief was that God was a creator who invented a mechanical universe that ran according to strict laws revealed in such mathematical principles as calculus. The result? That the complex motions of the heavens could be explained by mathematical laws was implicit proof of God's plan.

The Japanese, on the other hand, had no philosophical need to link science and the universe. They had an intermingled view of the universe, one in which God, nature, and human beings are bound together and are inseparable. As a result, the great Japanese mathematician's discoveries were largely ignored by his own people. They saw no practical use in figuring out the path of planets or other phenomena of the universe, whereas we use calculus to send rockets to the moon.

The children I have studied have an instinctive understanding of the new sciences, specifically because they were prepared to understand them as a result of their NDEs, a case of mystical truth leading to a better understanding of scientific truth. My patients are already speaking the language of the theoretical physicist or the chaos mathematician. They can understand an eternal universe in which time has several dimensions, and in which space, time, and mass cannot be separated. They have perceived the universe from a frame of reference outside their bodies and have experienced an encounter with a loving God.

One of the most dramatic examples of this scientific understanding is Olaf Swendon's NDE. Olaf, a Swedish inventor, did not trust the knowledge from his mystical vision until the discovery of the subatomic particles, the neutrinos, was made. When he learned of neutrinos, he realized he had already seen them in his teens when he nearly died.

Olaf is an early example of the budding paradigm. He had mystical insight, and yet lacked the academic knowledge that comes from studying organic chemistry and theoretical physics that needed to put his insight to work. Once he had intellectual foundation, he benefited enormously. He is a now multimillionaire and has more than one hundred patents in organic chemistry. But that's not all. His NDE has led to spiritual insights. He could have used his knowledge to make poison gas or weapons of war. Instead, he recognized that all of life is interconnected, that he had spiritual and philosophical responsibilities, so he invented a way to include more chalk in paper pulp. The result? More trees are saved.

At the "Beyond the Brain" conference at Cambridge University in 1995, the subliminal fear behind this emerging paradigm was best expressed by Dr. Julian Candy when he asked, "How do we abandon our central myth without sliding back into superstition?" By the central myth he means the old world view that the universe is simply a giant mechanical watch whose actions are predictable.

The new sciences have led to the development of nuclear power, and the potential of plentiful and cheap energy. We routinely view the inside of the human body to discover cancers and other illnesses or injuries by using nuclear magnetic resonance imaging, or MRI, which detects subtle variations in the electromagnetic properties of different types of body tissue. Almost every hospital now has an MRI, an incredible tool that aids in diagnosis, which was developed from scientific concepts that were theoretical only two decades ago.

I do not dispute the need for rigid science and skepticism. Still, our quest for the meaning of the universe and the nature of God must continue. At one time, the universe was thought by philosophers to be supported on the back of a giant turtle. Astrophysicist Stephen Hawking discussed this concept at a lecture, and was surprised when a woman got up and said she believed it.

"And what is under the turtle?" asked Hawking.

"Oh, that's easy," said the woman. "It's turtles all the way down."

This woman's answer was effective if not correct. We are no closer to answering the questions of the universe than the ancient philosophers. Who made the universe? What is outside the universe? How can a universe have anything outside it? Where did it come from in the first place? What happened before the Big Bang? The universe is rife with questions waiting to be answered, ones that may well change the notion that nature runs like clockwork.

This same thinking applies to our personal universe as well. There is much to know about the nature of our souls and exactly what it is that makes us tick. Like the universe around us, we too are a compendium of unanswered questions, many of them related to the so-called metaphysical aspects of ourselves. Do we survive bodily death? How does telepathy work? Can our souls leave our body and travel elsewhere? Is there a way to mentally access our own healing powers? Do we live again as other people?

These are all questions that we can begin to answer by examining the physiology of the NDE. Like the opening of a secret door into a new world, the NDE provides a new way in which to examine the link between our brains and the universe.

In that sense we are exploring a new paradigm, one in which science and spirituality join hands to help people on all sides of the mind-body argument find common ground.

I find it reassuring that science and religion are not only connected, but that they need one another. There is irony in this statement, I know, given the hostility of science toward spirituality. But the evidence tells us that a mechanistic computer model of the brain simply cannot explain human consciousness. Humans think in ways that aren't mechanistic and that are linked to forces that fit into our definition of "divine" or "spiritual." Human consciousness, unlike that of computers, is inherently irrational. Creative hunches and intuitive guesses are the stuff of human consciousness, with logic filling in the gaps and propping up the theories. Time and again there is scientific evidence that links the mind to the spontaneous healing of the body or—even more amazing—the brain to areas outside its home in the skull. Sprinkled throughout the scientific literature in a number of different disciplines are examples of "mind reading," telekinesis, healing through the laying on of hands, visionary encounters with people who have died, verifiable out-of-body experiences, and many other examples of why the brain is not a computer but an object that controls and communicates in ways still too mysterious for science to comprehend.

Many scientists don't like to admit this. One participant at a consciousness conference in London said it best when he angrily asserted, "If we accept that man might have a spirit, we will be turning our back on science and the last three hundred years. We will lose all we have accomplished."

Even in the face of such skepticism, prestigious universities like the University of Virginia and the University of Connecticut are exploring the perceived outer limits of consciousness with thoughtful, objective research and inquiry into NDEs. It is reassuring to know that a handful of brave explorers have caught sight of the emerging paradigm shift and are preparing to embrace it.

That embrace includes acceptance of a series of indisputable facts that are at the foundation of current NDE research:

- NDEs and many other "spiritual events" are real. We can, through scientific means, differentiate between mental illness, physical illness, substance-based altered consciousness, and legitimate spiritual experiences such as NDEs.

- Transformation is the common link between all spiritual experiences, including mystical states, out-of-body experiences, and NDEs.

- A common link between these mystical experiences exists in brain physiology but is not limited to or contained by that physiology. Much of what constitutes a mystical or paranormal experience might exist outside the human brain and come to us through a shared fabric of thought and memory.

The psychologist and researcher Charles Tart summed up near death and consciousness research nicely when he said: "What we need is not another definition of consciousness, nor an explanation, but a better map. Such a map would enable us to plot the course taken both by these exciting new avenues in consciousness research and by the traditional pathways, and thus not only to perceive where perhaps unexpectedly they converge and bridges may be built, but also to glimpse the destination to which they lead. And a map, after all, is what a paradigm provides."

LIFE IS BUT A DREAM

It was getting late now. The crickets were singing, accompanied by the frogs down at the pond where some of the kids were trying their hand at fishing. Some of the parents and I assembled firewood into a large pile and set it alight. There was a giant whoosh as the dry wood burst into flames and snapped hungrily at the emerging stars.

The bright light attracted the children, just as I knew it would. Many of them have told me that the light they saw during their NDEs is always with them. Sometimes it's just out of sight; at other times it bathes them with a deep sense of spiritual well-being.

It had been a terrific day, with great food, great company, exciting games, and even more exciting reports from the children who were in my study. Jonathan, a young man of Indian descent, and Jane, a social worker, were tuning up their instruments for some traditional around-the-campfire singing. Jonathan had been adopted into an American family and brought a uniquely multicultural view to his NDE. Jane, who was a painfully shy child when she described her NDE to me fifteen years ago, has developed into a young woman of immense courage and energy who devotes herself to working with dying cancer patients. They are both unique, yet they share the knowledge that in death there is a kind of life that none of us can even begin to imagine until it happens to us.

I made a few closing remarks, thanking everyone for coming. My wife and I accepted applause from our guests and the singing began. As I joined in the familiar round, I was amazed at the significance of the song's closing line: "Merrily, merrily, merrily, merrily, life is but a dream."

It is a dream, but life is also an adventure . . .

2

A Taste of Their Medicine

IF YOU WANT TO BRING THAT TRANSFORMING SPIRITUAL light into your life, if you want to know who you are and where you are going, if you want the same insights and transformation experienced by the children I have studied who have had brief encounters with that light during near death experiences, you can have it. The "Big Secret" is that there is no big secret.

You do not need to take up constant meditation, or join an ashram, or travel to a distant location on a spiritual quest. The real goal of a spiritual quest is to learn to communicate with yourself. Pay attention to your own thoughts and actions. Listen to your thoughts and analyze your emotions, asking yourself, *Why am I happy?* Or, *Why am I angry?* By understanding your motivations and why you do what you do, you will become "enlightened."

How do I know this? I know it because it happened to me. I was healed by the lessons I learned from children who had almost died.

MY STORY

About five years ago, I was diagnosed with chronic high blood pressure. The news frightened me, and I immediately began doing what so many patients with high blood pressure do, taking medication.

I also went into a deep depression and became a hypochondriac. After my wife would fall asleep at night, I would go to the living room to check my blood pressure. Of course, it was always elevated, since I was so filled with anxiety. Soon, I was on three different medications for high blood pressure, and it was still out of control. I began to hyperventilate unconsciously and was unaware that my anxiety caused me to breathe faster than usual. Of course, I took that as a sign that I was getting worse. Soon, I was on antianxiety medications plus high blood pressure medications. And still my blood pressure was too high.

My weight, always a problem for me, soared. At night, I would gorge myself, often having a second dinner, not even tasting the food, simply in a frenzy to do anything to give myself some relief from the pressures I was putting on myself.

I was at the end of what I could endure.

I tried praying again, but found no relief. The spiritual vision that had occurred at the end of my "prayer experiment" mentioned in the introduction did not return this time.

If only I could learn to live in harmony with this illness, then I would have no further problems, I thought. That was when I hit upon an idea: I would tap the ten secrets of happiness that I had compiled from my talks with hundreds of children who have had near death experiences. These "secrets" were the habits they had developed in their lives after their NDEs, the ones that help them to stay in touch with their inner light, that same transforming light they saw when they almost died.

I actually had a list of these secrets in the file cabinet where I kept much of my near death research. Most of them came from kids and adults I had talked to for a transformation study, a study to determine the ways in which near death experiences change people. As I scanned the list, I marveled at its simplicity. "Why haven't I been doing this all along?" I asked myself. The answer to that question was easy. The ten secrets seemed so obvious that I had forgotten them. Now, as I sat down at my desk and looked at the list before me, I felt relieved by the notion that my life would be transformed without having to have a near death experience of my own.

TEN SECRETS OF THE TRANSFORMED

1. *Exercise.* Do some form of enjoyable exercise every day for at least thirty minutes—walk in a park, play catch with your daughter, wrestle with your son, use a home treadmill while watching television. Give daily exercise the same priority that you would work. After a few weeks, exercise will become a part of your schedule that you won't want to miss.

   By getting up in the morning and jogging with my son, my entire pattern changed. I now spend more time with him. We have developed a camaraderie instead of my constantly nagging him about homework. I am more tired at night and less likely to stay up eating junk food.

2. *Patterns* (be here now). Pay attention to your life patterns. Keep a journal. Do active meditation, a form of meditation in which you acknowledge and comment on your thoughts and inner feelings. With active meditation, you address your concerns about such things as money, kids, marriage, and work instead of using passive meditation to silence your inner narrator.

Active meditation is especially good for obsessive thinking. Rather than trying to silence our internal narrator, active meditation gives the narrator center stage. So, instead of trying *not* to think about a disagreeable boss, you actually think about him or her, focusing on the source of conflict and trying to reach a solution to your problem.

3. *Family and relationships.* Eat breakfast and dinner with your family at least four times a week. Turn off the TV and talk to each other. Develop the habit of listening to others for at least fifteen minutes a day. It's hard at first, but here are some tips:

   • Let others finish their sentences before you start to think of your response.

   • Say such things as "How did you feel about that?" "Tell me more," or simply repeat the last few words they said to you, out loud, in a reflective way.

4. *Trust your inner vision and intuition.* Most people do not lack for spiritual experiences or intuitions. They lack the courage to believe them and therefore dismiss them.

5. *Service.* Help others on a weekly basis, even in simple ways. Give your wife a foot rub. Volunteer to be a soccer coach. Donate food to a food drive. One surefire cure for a sense of meaninglessness in life is to volunteer at a school, day-care center, or hospital.

6. *Financial planning.* Cut expenses. Pay at least 20 percent extra on your credit card debt each month. Over the years, this will lead to peace of mind, not just monetary savings.

Save money every month, even a small amount. When Einstein was asked about the greatest miracle in life, he replied, "Compound interest." Small amounts of money, saved on a regular basis, compound into enormous returns. What does this have to do with spiritual harmony? In our society, it is easier to find spiritual harmony when you have money in the bank and are not burdened with a lot of debt.

7. *Diet.* Children who have had NDEs eat more fresh fruits and vegetables than the rest of us. Meeting that spiritual light leads to good eating habits and, in turn, a longer, healthier life. Try to add one new vegetable a month to your diet as you subtract one fast food or snack food a week. Often, small changes can lead to successful lifelong weight loss. Diets rarely do.

8. *Meditation/prayer (talk to God).* Spend at least fifteen minutes a day allowing input from your right temporal lobe to come in. If you don't want to pray actively, or cannot think of anything to say, repeat a word over and over while lying in bed. This simple act "turns on" the right temporal lobe, your God Spot.

9. *Learn to love.* Often, when we think of love, we mean self-love. Real love means thinking of someone else, that person's needs and feelings. It is hard to love. Often, it involves giving and sharing, which doesn't come naturally to many of us. You can learn to love but it takes time and practice. I will spend thirty minutes a day jogging for my health. Spending thirty minutes a day "loving," however, is just as good for your health. There are simple ways to do it. Commenting favorably on someone's new haircut is one way to

make that person feel good. Another is to bring co-workers a treat in the morning, or ask them how their child ren are doing in a play they are performing in. These are simple acts of caring that can help us all break out of our isolation. I am reminded that this is one of the ways recommended by stress researchers to break out of the type-A mold that so many find themselves in, the one that makes us stressed out, hostile, and unhappy.

10. *Spirituality.* Rediscover your relationship with all parts of the universe. Pay attention to what is going on around you and see your place within it. This will act on many different levels— your relationships with other people, with the environment, and with God.

This means different things to different people. For some, reestablishing a relationship with the universe will mean going to church once a week. For others, it means going to the beach or sitting in the park. Each person has his own way of addressing spirituality. The idea of kneeling before a bed and praying is offensive to some people, who feel religion and spirituality have nothing in common. For others, religion is a conduit to the divine. Find what works for you and do not limit yourself. After all, there is more than one path to righteousness.

In fact, I have used these secrets to great effect in my own life, although I will admit that it is hard to stay in the "rut of good habits." It is easy to think of other things to do besides exercise, and it is always difficult to "live in the now" and not dwell on the past or worry about tomorrow.

First, I observed my life and kept a journal. I noticed I had no time for exercise but way too much time for useless worrying. I went to my health club and began to pay attention. I noticed that people who exercised in the morning were generally slimmer and fitter than the gym patrons who exercised later in the day. That prompted me to make one simple change—to exercise every morning.

I lost weight. I was sleepier at night and went to bed earlier, resulting in less worrying at night and fewer blood pressure checks.

I started listening to my children more and spending time with them no matter how tired I was. Often, I would hear a nagging voice in my head nattering on about my blood pressure. To stop my negative inner voices, I took my mind off them by playing games with my children or reading books.

My wife asked me to read a book, *Men Are from Mars, Woman Are from Venus*, by Dr. John Gray. I did and thought it applied more to her than to me. She asked me to talk about it with her. Soon we were talking about books every night. Before we knew it, our sex life had improved, and I had even less time to check my blood pressure and eat ice cream late at night.

I started to talk to God, and to listen. Instead of desperation prayers, I had dialogues with God, often in the car on my way to work. I would talk about my life. I did my own life review, as I knew that was part of an NDE. I thought of the people I had hurt. I asked them for forgiveness.

As I prayed, I realized that much of my stress was about my treatment of my brother-in-law, an alcoholic who died of complications of drug and alcohol abuse when he was my age. I was mean to him, often practicing "tough love" when a kind word would have been better.

Suddenly, as I talked to God I realized I had a secret fear that I would die because my brother-in-law did. It would be God's punishment for my treatment of him. I went to my mother-in-law and talked with her for the first time about my fears, and how sad I was over the way I had treated Chris. I spent time with her talking about the pain of living with an alcoholic, drug-addicted son. Soon, I felt closer to her than I ever had before.

I offered myself in service. I volunteered to coach softball for my son's teams. I gave money at church. I had more non-homework-related issues to talk about with my son and have grown even closer to him. Understanding the unhealthy patterns in my life led to a better diet and regular exercise.

About one year into this plan, a bizarre thing happened, something I can only consider to be an activation of my God Spot. I found myself in a waking-dream state in the middle of the night, with the vision of a friend standing at the foot of my bed! This friend, a woman, was looking at me with a divine serenity on her face. Even in my dream state, where anything can happen, I was surprised to see her.

"Melvin, I have a gift for you," she said, extending her hand toward me. As she did, I felt my abdomen radiate with a bright, white light. I saw tissue burning hot and angry in the light, turning into soot, then washing away. Beautiful, healthy skin was left behind.

And then I awoke.

COMMUNICATION WITH GOD

I went to lunch with that friend several weeks later, and asked her about the dream without giving her any details. Since the experience was so vivid, I thought that maybe she'd had some kind of experience at the same time.

As it turned out, she had not had a dream or a spiritual vision, but she suggested that the vision gave me a metaphor for healing myself.

It is strange how that dream affected me. My blood pressure

became normal and I was able to stop taking two powerful blood pressure medications. Then I realized there was another positive side effect of my new life. The asthma that had plagued me for so many years had abated, along with my hypertension. Slowly, I weaned myself from the four medications I had been taking to control my asthma.

WHAT HAPPENED?

With the changes I had made, I had created a fertile ground for the universe to enter my life. I opened my right temporal lobe to communicate with God, waited patiently, and was rewarded. I spent time every day firmly in the present and periodically turned off my internal narrator. I learned again to love my family, to stop thinking only of my disease, my death, my heavy workload, my problems. I made it a point to listen to my daughter singing a silly song or to play checkers with my son.

After several years of having persistent hypertension, I became entirely normal. I have stayed that way for four years now. My blood pressure is normal and I do not take any medications. I haven't lost a lot of weight, but I am happy with my body and jog every day with my son.

At forty-six, I finally learned the secrets of living, from children who nearly died.

LESSONS OF THE LIGHT

Having used these ten secrets successfully in my own life, I began using them in my practice of pediatric medicine.

So often parents bring their children to me for their behavioral problems. They see typical teenage behavior as a complex problem when all too often the solutions are straightforward and simple.

For example, I had a severely depressed teenage patient

whose parents were considering divorce after twenty-five years of marriage. They were both were on Zoloft, and they brought in their son Adam so he could start taking an antidepressant too.

With little prodding, Adam began to talk about his life. He was tired most of the time, he said, and he hated school and hated his home life. The only pleasure in his life, he said, was a part-time job working at a fast-food restaurant. Other than that, life was all drudgery. He had lost twenty-five pounds in the last year.

I thought he was a perfect candidate for an antidepressant, and I began talking to him about the different medications he could take and what he could expect in the way of side effects. He suddenly held up his hand in a defiant way and asked, "Why does everyone always look to a pill for the solution to their problems? It's just the easy way out."

"Okay," I said, "let's look at the alternatives. Studies have shown that for patients who are chronically fatigued, regular exercise, like walking right before bed, is very effective in enhancing normal sleep and preventing daytime fatigue. In fact, one study looked at exercise as compared to using mood-altering medications and found exercise was more beneficial. So, let's figure out how we can factor exercise into your schedule."

I talked with the entire family about the value of exercise in fighting depression, and they all decided to give it a try. They started walking together in the evening, and as they did, their creativity as a family began expressing itself. Sometimes they just walked and made small talk. Other times they worked on solving their financial problems. Sometimes they just walked in silence. These family walks started a process of healing for them.

Six months later, the parents were still married. The mother, whose weight had been a problem, had lost twenty pounds and Adam's weight was stable. Most telling is the fact that both parents are off medication, and they speak of their problems as solvable.

About 60 percent of medical problems are considered diseases of lifestyle by the National Institutes of Health and could be solved with simple changes like exercising more and eating less.

The secret to a healthy, spiritual life is oftentimes as easy as a simple change in lifestyle. Yet many people overlook the obvious problems in their lives because they don't seem to have anything to do with spirituality or peace of mind. Instead, they ignore their excessive weight, or depression, or burgeoning drinking or smoking problem and hope for that mystical flash of light that will put them in touch with their own spirituality.

They have forgotten—or maybe never knew—that the search for spiritual health is all about achieving balance in their lives. Indeed, one of the precepts of spiritual healing—physical or mental—is achieving balance, one step at a time, until your body is in a harmony as close to perfect as it can get.

Invitation to Explore

You could easily stop reading now and improve your spiritual life by following the ten lessons of near death experiencers. Or, you could find that your curiosity is aroused and you want to know more about the God Spot, that place in our brain where God lives. That is what happened to me. I began to wonder about how this mysterious area of the brain could be made more accessible, and what would happen if it *were* more accessible.

Why, I wondered, was the God Spot a part of human physiology? Had past cultures used it to speak to God, and had it gone dormant as we became busier with other pursuits? Does it connect us to the fabric of the universe? Is the God Spot the source of the "meaning of life" that everyone is always seeking? Is it the part of us that lives on after the physical body dies?

One night not long after my hypertension had been brought under control, I began to outline a series of essays that I wanted to write about that place in all of us where God lives. These essays would explore—through scientific research, philosophy, and personal experience—an array of important issues about the area of the brain that is activated during NDEs and mystical experiences. These questions are the most important in the field of near death studies and have rarely been looked at in depth by any one individual. Rather, these questions have been broken into dozens of pieces, each one the subject of scientific study or discourse. Soon, I realized that I was on a path no one before me had taken, one that would present a unified theory of how and why mystical experiences take place and—more important—what happens when they do.

Within a few hours, I had outlined a number of questions that would be answered by these essays:

- Can memory exist outside the body? This would seem to be a shocking question, yet no modern scientific or medical theory currently explains memory and where (or how) it is stored.

    I was speaking at UCLA to a group of neuroscientists when the subject of the location of memory first presented itself as a valid question. A physician in the audience pointed out that if comatose patients can have NDEs and remember them, then we need to explain how a dying, dysfunctional brain can process a long-term memory. I knew from my transformation study that children not only remember their NDEs, they remember them all of their lives.

One simple answer is that perhaps memories are not stored in the brain. Although an outrageous statement, if true it would answer many questions associated with perception, including ghosts, angels, the origin of past lives, even false memory syndrome, in which people "remember" childhood events that never happened to them.

- Is reincarnation the act of "tapping in" to a universal memory bank? I had always discounted past-life memories as weird or flaky. I was unaware of the mainstream researchers like Dr. Ian Stevenson of the University of Virginia. When I read his research, I found an enormous number of excellent studies. But there was one flaw: There was not a theory to explain how past-life information can be contained in the brain of a living person.

I had many questions about past lives, arising from my own patients. For example, a two-and-a-half-year-old patient in my practice told both me and his mother, in great detail, about a past life. He was too young to be inventing stories or fantasizing, he had only just learned to talk. He must have been remembering something, but what?

My theory that memories might be stored outside the brain offers a new way of understanding reincarnation and past-life memories.

- Are ghosts and angels really "trapped" energy patterns? The perception of angels and ghosts involves encounters with beings that seem to be from another reality. Angels allow actual communications and interactions with the universe, whereas ghosts seem more static. In my work, I have concluded that both angels and ghosts are perceived through our right temporal lobes. But what is the right temporal lobe perceiving?

The theoretical physicists that I work with at Los Alamos, and the National Institute of Discovery Science, have explained to me that the energy we give off in the form of thought and behavior does not disappear but survives somewhere in nature. If that is true, perhaps our energy becomes a part of that universal memory bank, perceivable at times as ghosts or angels by our right temporal lobes.

• Is there a type of person who can communicate with this universal memory bank more easily than the rest of us? I have hypothesized that our right temporal lobe is our biological means of communicating with God as well as communicating with a universal memory. If this is so, it would follow that some people are more right-temporal-lobe "gifted" than others. In studying people who seem to have extraordinary right-temporal-lobe talents, I have learned they have frequently had NDEs or spiritual visions as children or young adults, which triggered their mystical talents. Is it possible that having a near death experience could actually activate the right temporal lobe?

The transformation study, an examination of adults who had near death experiences as children, would indicate that this is true. We learned from this study that adults who had NDEs as children had four times the number of verifiable psychical experiences as people who have never had NDEs. Could it be that having a near death experience allows people suddenly to realize an entire area of their brain that they have not been using?

That was certainly the case with Joe McMonagle, who had an NDE while serving in the army. Now he is one of the star remote viewers for the Central Intelligence Agency (CIA), a man who successfully drew the physical layout of a secret Soviet missile installation he envisioned in his mind while sitting in a windowless room in California.

• Is there such a thing as coincidence? This might seem a silly question, since we see them all the time. With me, they often revolve around illness. When a child becomes seriously ill, for example, a trivial event in the family's life will be seen as having triggered the illness. One patient recently started preschool and was then diagnosed with leukemia. The parents felt that cause and effect were involved. Something at the preschool, these parents believed, clearly caused the leukemia.

Yet the child had had leukemia for many months before the diagnosis was made, and the illness clearly started well before the child entered the preschool. Yet I could not convince the parents of this fact. In their anger and grief, they became fixated on the idea that some environmental hazard at the school had caused the leukemia. This is an example of magical thinking, or the search for meaning in one's life gone wrong. It also illustrates the powerful need we have to find connections and attach meaning to every important thing that happens in our life.

So the question "Is there such a thing as coincidence?" really refers to a deeper question: "Do we, as human beings, create meaning for ourselves in an otherwise random and incomprehensible universe, or is there a pattern to life that we can find if we are aware and patient enough?"

When children tell me that they learned from their near death experience that "there are no coincidences"—and they commonly do—they mean that they learned that life has a pattern and an innate meaning beyond what we, as human beings, impose upon it.

My question is whether or not this is a scientific concept as well as a spiritual one. Are these children making a sound scientific statement as well as a profound spiritual one when they tell me that all of life has purpose and meaning and that there are no coincidences? This is a question that scientists like Albert Einstein and Richard Feynman struggled with from a purely scientific perspective. I hope to contribute to the study of this important question.

• And what is intuition, anyway? We all speak casually of our inner voice, of the "gut instincts" of our conscience. No less an authority than Gavin de Becker, a security expert who has guarded several U.S. presidents, has written in *The Gift of Fear* that we trivialize and dismiss one of our most important senses—our own intuition. He feels that learning to use one's intuition is more important than body armor and a gun.

When I started in medicine, my professors would say, "There is one thing that we cannot teach you; we cannot teach you to trust your instincts, to listen to what your gut tells you." Now I wondered: Is intuition a blend of psychic talents such as telepathy, remote viewing, precognition (seeing the future), and direct communication with God all blended together to give us the insights we call intuition?

Also, does my research on children's NDEs indicate that perhaps we can train ourselves to use our "gut" in a more conscious way? Researchers have speculated that primitive humans were far more adept than we are at remote viewing, telepathy, and precognition. Perhaps as we became more left-temporal-lobe-based, the area of the brain where language is located, we forgot our right-temporal-lobe skills.

Having used the Ten Secrets of the Transformed with my own hypertension and high blood pressure, my mind turned to questions of healing, namely:

• Why do prayers help some people who are seriously ill? There are several excellent studies proving the power of prayer. The best known of these was done in the late 1980s by Randolph Byrd, a cardiologist at San Francisco General Hospital. His study, the first serious research into the medical effects of prayer, found that heart patients who were prayed for healed 10 percent better and faster than patients who were not prayed for. A total of 393 patients were in his highly controversial study.

The Byrd study was repeated in 1998 by doctors at Kansas City's Mid-America Heart Institute using 990 patients. Their findings were practically the same as Byrd's: The prayed-for patients healed 11 percent faster and better than those not prayed for.

A study that has been replicated is difficult to dismiss, although many doctors wish it could be. If the only variable is prayer, then prayer can be considered medicine, right? This is difficult for many doctors to grasp, since it is a form of healing that does not involve giving a patient medicine.

I have long believed that every cell in our body has a pattern of energy, a "morphic form," that determines such factors as its size, shape, and health. Modern biological theory holds that our DNA is a holographic reflection of a deeper energy field that exists in nature, a pattern that gives us and all things the form that we have.

I was excited by the notion that prayer can affect this morphic form and I looked forward to exploring that aspect of healing.

- How are mystical experiences like prayer? I also knew that mystical experiences have a profound healing effect on the body. In studies of people who have had miraculous healings from cancer and autoimmune diseases, an NDE, out-of-body, or similar experience is almost always involved. And, people who have been documented as having healing abilities almost always have an NDE or other mystical experience in their past.

All of this indicated that the right temporal lobe is involved in somehow regulating the healing experience by communicating with the body's "morphic forms," or healing energy. My goal would be to explore how such a thing could work.

PATH TO EXPLORATION

In looking at the list of questions I would be exploring, I realized that many of the likely answers seemed to be theoretical, and even impractical. Like the prayer research of Dr. Byrd, these questions represented a fringe area of study that some doctors feel is better left outside the medical arena. Still, I knew from personal experience how that arena can shift. When I conducted research into the transformative nature of NDEs, I was considered to be in a fringe area. Now, that research is considered both mainstream and medically valuable.

As I examined the list of questions I would explore, Jean-Baptiste-Joseph Fourier came to mind. This eighteenth-century French mathematician and Egyptologist spent the last decade of his life developing an analytical theory of heat. Fourier's work, from which we are benefiting today, led to great advances in the field of mathematical physics, including medical diagnosis instruments and weather prediction. At the time, however, it seemed to have almost no use at all. One day, he was asked by a colleague, "What use is this Fourier series [of mathematical equations], anyway?" To which Fourier replied, "What use is a child, until we see him grow up to be a man?"

So it is with many of these questions. I knew the answers in my essays might amount to only baby steps, but they were steps nonetheless, and ones that would lead down the road to personal discovery.

3

The Anatomy of Memory

CAN MEMORY EXIST OUTSIDE THE BODY? CAN MEMORY BE stored outside the brain? Can we tap into these memories, reaching them the way we might access a personal website on the World Wide Web? All the cutting-edge research says yes, which helps explain cases like Phil. To this day, he casts a distrustful eye on his NDE, in part because his memory of the event that led to his NDE, and the NDE itself, has faded.

He insists, "But if I was dead, how could I remember what happened to me? It must have been a dream!" He was ten when the car his parents were driving in plunged off an icy bridge and into a river below. His father was killed.

Phil was a good example of the maxim we used when I worked for Airlift Northwest, a helicopter rescue service: "If they're not warm and dead, they're not dead." This grizzly axiom refers to the protective mechanisms that cold water has on the body and the brain. When people fall into cold water, their body often shunts blood to the brain, leaving parts of their body cold and without blood so that the brain stays warm and functioning. Because of this phenomenon, miracles such as the one experienced by Phil sometimes happen, and a full recovery occurs, even though the person has been underwater for at least twenty minutes.

Indeed, Phil did survive after nearly drowning and having complete cardiac arrest. Shortly after the tragedy, he described his NDE to me in great detail. Now, it's a blank slate upon which the words "world-class skeptic" are firmly etched.

He continues to insist he "just had a dream," not an NDE. He lists reasons why his NDE was not real. First, he didn't go down a tunnel, he went down a big noodle, "not a spiral noodle, just a regular old noodle, long and straight . . . and it had a rainbow in it!" Second, he said he didn't "meet God or Jesus, just a bee and a bunch of flowers." In fact, he wasn't even in human heaven at all, but somehow wound up in "animal heaven" where he also saw his grandmother. For Phil, that clinched it, since his grandmother was already dead! "And anyway," he added, "mostly, dead people can't remember things, so it must have been a dream."

Phil has put his finger on one of the most troubling aspects of the NDE. If these experiences really do occur with dying, often comatose patients, how is it then that they can process any memories of the experience at all?

Another of my patients, Mardy, can't explain how she's retained the details of her NDE, but she has. She was just eight when she slipped into a diabetic coma in an emergency room. Yet she can describe how, as the coma deepened and she edged closer to death, she eased out of her body and became engaged in conversation by shining beings.

These shining beings gave her a choice of pushing a green button or a red button. She thought that pushing the red one would keep her from returning to her mother and the life she knew, so she pressed the green one. Instantly, she returned to her body.

What my patients remember of these events as young adults, in what degree of detail they can recall their NDEs and the way those recollections affect their lives today, varies widely. It isn't surprising. These were traumatic events that occurred at an age when, in many cases, consciousness and a sense of self were still being formed.

A MEMORY MANUAL

There is no coherent theory of how memory works. Our knowledge of memory is a little like being in a huge black cave with a tiny penlight. The light illuminates only a minute proportion of the cave's full expanse. Enormous areas remain unseen, uncharted, and unknown. The basics of how memories are stored, processed, and recalled are so mysterious that the late Karl Lashley, a psychologist who studied memory his entire professional life, said, "If I didn't know better, I would think that memory is stored outside of the brain." He said this after watching lab rats with 90 percent of their brains removed run the same mazes as well as they had with them 100 percent intact.

We know that memory has to do with the right and left temporal lobes of the brain because damage to those areas interferes with long- and short-term memories. Furthermore, electrical stimulation studies of the temporal lobes and the hippocampus show that vivid, three-dimensionally perceived memories can be elicited when these areas are stimulated. Yet, curiously, the same memory cannot be evoked by stimulating the same area twice. Apparently, it's a little like randomly starting a CD or a cassette tape. You can never be sure where you are on the recording.

Although we know little about how memory is stored,

there are some basics about memory that we do know. There appear to be two basic forms of memory, short term and long term. Short-term memory lasts up to about six hours and is transient. If short-term memories aren't encoded into long-term memory, they vanish.

When people have NDEs, the opposite frequently happens. NDE research strongly suggests that as we progress deeper into a coma, and come closer to death, the ability to process memories seems to intensify. Inexplicably, this occurs at a point of extreme brain dysfunction. Memories might return because the right temporal lobe is activated at the point of death, which causes it to link to a universal memory bank, one that possibly exists outside the body.

This phenomenon of right-temporal-lobe activation has been documented in fighter pilots who are subjected to strong gravitational (G) forces in centrifuges in preparation for the physiological rigors of flying fighter planes. When the centrifuge runs reach six to eight G forces, pilots lose consciousness. This causing of a loss of consciousness is intentional and is done to test loss of consciousness on the pilots' abilities.

This loss of blood to the brain triggers the same areas of the brain that are activated during a near death experience. Pilots who black out from these G-forces report such experiences as being out of their bodies, and seeing family, friends, and even dead relatives. They report having pleasant sensations of peace, and often say that they no longer fear death, just like children and adults who have lost blood flow to their brains as a result of illness or trauma. Just like people who have had real NDEs, these pilots retain the memory of these sensations. They have even memorialized the experience with a patch that shows a skeleton wearing a flight helmet and pointing down a long tunnel of light.

THE NDE-MEMORY CONNECTION

The nature of memory is one of the most challenging aspects of NDEs. If NDEs occur to dying, often comatose patients who have severe physiological derangements of their brain chemistry, how is it that they can process any memory of the experience? After all, the gods I worshiped in medical school, the brilliant neurologists Fred Plum and Michael Posner, wrote, "Coma wipes clean the slate of consciousness." Period. No exceptions. End of discussion.

Despite the insistence of the existing scientific community, the question continues to beg explanation. If someone's brain isn't functioning, then how can he or she have memory?

Virtually every authority on consciousness agrees—consciousness and memory are interlinked. Modern scientific thought is increasingly exploring the notion that memories can exist independent of brain function. It's an intriguing possibility, and one of the few that offers answers rather than more questions.

AT THE LEVEL OF NEURONS

The reigning theory of memory is the concept of the "neural network." Boggled by the complexity of the human brain, physiologists turned to such simple nervous systems as those found in the lowly sea slug to learn the mystery of short-term memory. The sea slug has a very simple, primitive nervous system. It responds to light or electrical stimulation. By careful analysis of the chemical transmitters at the level of communication, or the "synapses" between the neurons, it has been shown that the patterns and percentages of these chemicals actually change in response to repeated stimulation, and that those changes seem to correspond to learned behavior on the part of the slug. These changes seem to dissipate after six to eight hours, which is similar to short-term memory storage.

Researchers assume that a more complex version of this neural network exists in the brains of higher animals.

The most persuasive proponent of neural networks as the building blocks of consciousness is Nobel Prize winner Francis Crick. He wrote the book *The Astonishing Hypothesis* about neural networks and consciousness, in which he states, "The speculations . . . are not a fully worked-out coherent set of ideas. Rather, they constitute work in progress. I believe the correct way to conceptualize consciousness has not yet been discovered. What has been discussed in this book [neural networks, etc.] has very little to do with the human soul . . . language . . . mathematics or problem solving in general." This illustrates how little is known about memory.

OUTSIDE LOOKING IN

There is another approach to the concept of memory, one that says that memory is packaged and stored outside the human brain. By postulating that memories are stored outside the human brain, we can arrive at a coherent theory of memory that explains the clinical data and resolves many of the contradictions.

I further propose that the right temporal lobe is, as Penfield stated, the "interpretive cortex," the area that packages memories and assembles the various elements that make up the change in the neural material responsible for memory, or the "memory engram." It is not, in this theory of remote memory, a system that always stores memory within the brain. Rather, it is a transmitter and receiver, communicating directly with a source of memory that exists outside the human brain.

As odd as it may seem, this theory is compatible with modern scientific thinking.

Support is found in the work of Dr. Karl Pribram, who investigated memory when attempting to unravel the functioning of the human brain. In the 1940s, it was thought that memory was coded as "engrams," complex bits of information including such things as the smell of a rose, the feeling of a kiss, and verbal and visual images of family and friends. It was assumed that engrams would turn out to be coded on specific neurons or by complex interactions of neurons and neuro-chemicals.

Pribram summarized in writing thirty years of memory research. His writings revealed, among other things, that removing parts of animals' brains did not result in the loss of memory.

Meanwhile, Pribram was realizing the same thing on his own human patients who had had areas of their brains removed in an effort to control epilepsy. To his great surprise, he found that the memory of these patients was seldom impaired. By the 1960s, Pribram became convinced that memory was distributed throughout the brain, and that each part of the brain contained all its memories.

This became Pribram's holographic theory, a belief that each piece of an object contains the pattern for the entire object. Pribram showed that portions of the brain work in the same fashion. He found, for instance, that vision in rats seems to be processed holographically. With more than 90 percent of their optic nerves severed, rats can still see.

Pribram devised a series of experiments to show conclusively that there is not even a one-to-one correspondence between what we think we see and the electrical activity of neurons in our eyes. He concluded that our eyes construct our model of reality and that they are less like video cameras than we think. He wrote, "These experimental results are incompatible with the view that a photo-like image becomes projected onto the cortex [during the process of seeing]."

We have been looking for memory in the hardwiring of the

brain, in the actual neurons themselves, or the specific neuro-transmitters acting between neurons. In Pribram's theory, memory and other brain processes occur not only in the communication between neurons, but in the endless ripples and patterns of energy that crisscross each other within the brain. The neurons in the brain generate an endless and kaleidoscopic array of patterns. This is the source of the brain's holographic properties and the storage area of memories.

"The hologram was there all the time in the . . . nature of brain cell connectivity," observed Pribram. "We simply didn't have the wit to realize it." This model explains the vastness of memory, which has been estimated to be able to store a staggering amount of information. The brain has some 100 million neurons, many with 100,000 or more connections to send signals to other neurons. The number of potential pathways is far beyond the ability of the most advanced computers.

This accounts for our ability to recall *and* forget. Memory is analogous to shining a laser beam on a piece of film in order to find a certain image. Often, our internal laser beam is slightly off. This results in the frustrating occurrence of knowing that you know a name or a place, but not being able to recall it.

It also accounts for associative memory. Based on the holographic concept of memory storage, multiple images and events can be simultaneously processed and superimposed over one another, creating another layer of complexity. For example, the brain-wave pattern for an easy chair could be superimposed over the pattern for the verbal memories of the text of a newspaper superimposed over the visual image of a picture in the paper. So, when a person sees an easy chair, the entire pattern is recalled, evoking the memory of reading something in the paper.

Physicist Pieter van Heerden discovered a phenomenon known as "interference holography," which demonstrates that holograms store not only images, but such concepts as similarities and differences between images. This important concept explains how we can perceive that someone's face almost looks like your brother's face, but isn't.

SUPPORT FOR THEORY

Pribram's theories have received considerable experimental and mathematical support. Indiana University biologist Paul Pietsch demonstrated that when a salamander's brain was removed from its body, it remained alive but in a stupor. When its brain was returned, it would return to normal activity. It didn't seem to matter how the brain was returned. He could reverse the hemispheres, implant it upside down, return only small pieces; he could shuffle it, dice it, flip it, and mince it, and still the salamander behaved normally as long as some part of its brain in some configuration was present.

Mathematical support for these concepts is found in Fourier forms, named after the eighteenth-century mathematician Jean-Baptiste-Joseph Fourier, who created mathematical equations that could convert complex waveforms into visual images and back again. His theories are the mathematical equivalent of the process that occurs when, in a television set, a video camera translates an image into electromagnetic frequencies and back again. Physicist Dennis Gabor used Fourier's forms to demonstrate the mathematics behind the hologram. For his work, he was given a Nobel Prize in 1971.

In 1979, Berkeley neurophysiologists Russel and Karren DeValois demonstrated that the high-order processing cells in the brain's visual system respond not to individual signals from individual receptors on the retina, but rather to a seemingly disorganized pattern of signals that were shown mathematically to represent Fourier forms. Their research revealed that the language of the brain is the language of complex ripples of interference that can be mathematically decoded to represent images, sounds, and sensations.

If the brain is a hologram and perceives the world in mathematical and holographic terms, and even our bodies obey the language of mathematics, what is the world actually made of? What is the reality our eyes see, not the reality that our brain perceives and re-creates according to mathematical dictates?

Physicist Nick Herbert used this analogy to address the dilemma: "The world is a radically ambiguous and ceaselessly flowing quantum soup behind our backs. Every time we quickly turn to 'see' the soup, it freezes, and it turns into ordinary reality. Humans can never experience the true texture of quantum reality, because everything we touch turns to matter."

According to modern physics, what we consider to be real is no more real than a video-game screen. On the surface of the screen, two people might seem to be playing tennis, each hitting the ball to the other. Actually, there is a deeper program that is sensing mathematical signals from the operators and translating them into the movement of the people and the ball. In fact, the people on the video game are not hitting the ball at all, but, rather, the entire game is a response to the actions of a deeper program.

In terms of our theory of extra-cerebral memory, which is memory that exists outside the body, it is clear that there is plenty of storage space for memories in the endlessly changing patterns of subatomic life. Every inch of space contains the energy of a trillion atom bombs and has the capacity to store the information of all the computers on earth.

This view of the world is summarized by science writer Michael Talbot: "Our brains mathematically construct objective reality by interpreting frequencies that are ultimately projections from another dimension, a deeper order of existence that is beyond both space and time. The brain is a hologram enfolded in a holographic universe."

NEW UNDERSTANDING

The real story is far more complex and is a starting point for a new understanding of how the brain works. John Archibald Wheeler, a Princeton physicist, is one of the most eloquent thinkers of this new understanding of brain and mind. He believes that we live in a participatory universe, one in which life and mind are woven into the fabric of the universe. In this theory, memories are stored all around us. They are stored in the patterns of life, the same patterns we see as trees or hear as birds' songs.

My theory allocates only short-term memory to the actual workings of the brain. Short-term memory depends on electrochemical interactions in neurons. These short-term memories, as well as all sensations, thoughts, images, and motor functions of the brain, are being sorted continually and processed by a portion of our brain known as the hippocampus, then blended with old memories and emotions by the limbic system. Then memory is transferred to the right temporal lobe, where, I speculate, it is linked to the universal patterns of energy that surround us and make up the universe.

There are a number of specific assumptions about memory we can make by using this theory, some of which future scientific research will no doubt address. They include:

• Infants and fetuses should be able to process memories. Conventional neurobiological theory does not allow for the existence of prenatal and infant memories, even though there is a large amount of clinical data demonstrating the existence of such memories.

- All memories are a complex mixture of real and false memories. This includes the life review associated with NDEs. Future experiments can be done to determine if the memories of the life review are more accurate than other types of memory.

- Memories of past lives have a common source. People who have past-life experiences may be tapping into the "memory fabric" of the universe, or some other outside-the-body source of memory.

The possible existence of a universal "memory fabric" explains how, in an NDE life review, all the memories, feelings, and sensations are experienced simultaneously. These and all other memories are stored together. It also explains why different memories are retrieved when the same spot in the right temporal lobe is stimulated again and again. The right temporal lobe is more a receiver/transmitter than a storage facility. Stimulating the same spot repeatedly leads to a different image each time, similar to turning a television on and off again and again.

Information storage in holographic forms is fundamental to the universe. Time, say some physicists, is not. They tell us that time does not exist and everything that ever has or will happen is happening all at once as part of the memory fabric of the universe.

Research on this topic is further reinforced by the children who have told us that such a memory fabric exists as a sort of "house of God," and that visiting it was part of their NDE.

It is not a great leap of logic to comprehend a universal memory that exists free of the constraints of time and as part of an evolving universal consciousness. It simply represents a reinterpretation of the clinical information we currently have about memory.

Neuroscientists accept that the brain and the body are bio-electrochemical in nature, but we have tended to ignore the electromagnetic aspects of neurochemistry. The brain is constantly generating endless patterns and currents of electromagnetic energy. I am suggesting that patterns of energy are formed by those currents and that these patterns interface with a universal energy pattern that underpins, at the subatomic level, all of reality.

What the physicists and children tell us is, in fact, actually true: There is a timeless, all-knowing space through which we have access to memory or mystical insights. For some reason, the dying brain comes in contact with this memory fabric. People who recover from a brush with death usually find that many behavior patterns have been changed. They want different jobs or new families, for example. Their reset switch was pressed by their encounter with the universal energy pattern. They were transformed and imbued with a new potential. They were, in essence, transformed by the mystical light.

4

Do Souls Have Memory?

A PERPLEXED COUPLE BROUGHT THEIR FOUR-YEAR-OLD daughter to see me. For almost a year, since the age of three, the young girl had been talking about her "other mother." As she put it: "I don't mean you, Mommy, I mean before you."

The girl had been convincingly telling her dumbfounded parents about what they believed was a past life, one in which their daughter had been born in a place where everyone had brown or black skin. She told them she was very old and walked with a limp. Some other old people where she lived were partially paralyzed, and couldn't move parts of their faces or half of their bodies.

She gave detailed descriptions of her life as an elderly woman in a village in Africa and how, when she died, she turned into a ball of light and eventually came out of her new mommy's tummy.

I had the parents bring back the girl several times during the next year. By the age of five, she no longer remembered anything about her reported past life and did not speak of it anymore.

I had heard another such story of a four-year-old child remembering what seemed to be a past life. The mother said that ever since the child could first talk, she would talk about her other mother and father. She said she lived in a big house and had a big backyard. She said her father was a pilot and was very old and that her other mother was nice. She described many details of her other life, a typical American one in a suburban community.

Though she could not provide details that could be independently verified—her name, her parents' names, the street address, the city they lived in, how she died in her other life—the story seemed to be more than the product of an active imagination.

The child would often bring up her other parents and wonder if they missed her. She was very matter-of-fact about it and did not seem to get any secondary gain from the story. Her parents, who were Presbyterians, and occasional churchgoers, did not believe in reincarnation.

What is remarkable about these children's stories is how prosaic they are. Adults who say they have past-life memories often claim lives that have some dramatic theme—having been a pharaoh's slave or a nobleman in ancient Rome. These children's stories were very different in their matter-of-factness.

Past-life regression techniques that assist individuals in bringing memories from a past life to consciousness have emerged in recent years. Scientists and theologians generally dismiss them as fantasy, overactive imagination, or just plain lies. On the other hand, those who are willing to acknowledge that there is much we don't know about memory are taking a close look at past-life reports with an eye for how they may fit into the puzzle known as memory.

The Mystery of Past Lives

Other aspects of this phenomenon deserve further research as well. For instance, there are cases of two different children living in different cities who have been reported as remembering the same past life. Since they couldn't both have been the same person in a past life, this could only happen if they somehow tapped in to that person's memory bank after he or she had died.

Sometimes the volume and depth of detail recalled is so baffling that one must at least consider that there is more than randomness at work. Take the case reported by the Oxford-trained British psychologist Sir Cyril Burt. While studying hypnosis, he hypnotized a blind philosophy student at Oxford.

One evening, while under hypnosis, the student started to speak in an unfamiliar voice. He stated that he was an Egyptian carpenter who carved certain tablets in the tomb of "the king in his den." He described an eagle, a hand, a zigzag, and a god on the steps wearing a bright white crown that designated him as the king of upper and lower Egypt. The carpenter/philosophy student then gave a vivid, detailed description of the inner tomb.

Eight months later, Sir Cyril Burt learned from newspaper reports that at the time of the hypnosis interview, Sir Flinders Petrie had been excavating the tomb of a king of the first dynasty in Egypt whose name was Semti (3200 B.C.) and whose mystical name was Den. Den Semti was the first Egyptian ruler to assume the title of "king of upper and lower Egypt." He was often called the "God of the Steps" and wore an emblematic white crown. This find was not reported to the press until eight months after the student had described, under hypnosis, the tomb.

Many cases of past-life regression involve the subject's providing details of a past life and then the investigator's attempting to verify these details by studying the historical record. The problem with these cases is the suspicion that somehow the subject studied those same historical records either as part of a conscious hoax or as unconscious recall of repressed memories. Often, the details are so vague that motivated investigators, if they look long enough, can find something remotely similar in the historical record.

The next case is unique in that it involves objective, independent historians who actually participated in the study. Hypnotic sessions were conducted by Loring Williams, an expert practitioner of past-life regressions, on a fifteen-year-old New Hampshire boy named George Field.

Each time he was regressed, George became a Civil War–era farmer from North Carolina named Jonathan Powell who claimed to have been killed, as he would often say, by "damned Yankees." George recounted the geography of his town, Jefferson, the names of his relatives, and the location of a nearby Quaker church. He supplied details, and during one session named the county in which Jefferson was located and the positions and names of the main roads in town.

The hypnotist took George to North Carolina, where he had never been. There, they enlisted the cooperation of the Jefferson town historian. The historian sat in on the hypnosis sessions and asked questions such as "Do you know Jonathan Baker?" George answered, "Yeah, I have met him a number of times. He's got quite a bit of money and he always talks about it. I think he's got quite a few slaves." George's answers were so accurate that even the skeptical historian was stumped.

As Jonathan, George identified many other names of residents, including their occupations, where they lived, and the individuals' financial status. He recounted details concerning his own death, stating that he had been killed by Union soldiers wearing gray uniforms. The historian said it was a common practice for marauding Union soldiers to conceal their identities by wearing Rebel uniforms when plundering North Carolina.

The final detail of the case came after it was published in *Fate* magazine. A subscriber wrote to say that she was a great-niece of Jonathan Powell and that, in fact, he had been killed by Union soldiers. Researchers regard this as a nearly airtight case for the proof of reincarnation. I think it is also an airtight case for the existence of a universal memory bank, a place where all memory is stored.

CONFIRMED AND ACCURATE

Another past-life story that has withstood rigorous research is that of Kumkum Verma, a woman born in 1955 in Bahera, a town in northern India. She began speaking of her past life at about age three, declaring that she had previously lived in the nearby town of Urdu Bazar.

She died, she said, when her daughter-in-law poisoned her. Her past-life memories were very clear, including the names of her children and her in-laws, as well as a wealth of other details. Her birth parents were skeptical but carefully documented her statements and generated a written record of her claims. The report included a description of her home, the presence of an iron safe, a pet cobra, and mango orchards near her home. Because she was so young she often lacked the vocabulary to describe things and would pantomime them. For example, her son was a blacksmith, which she described with the gestures of using a hammer and bellows.

By age six, after a written, detailed record of the memories had been recorded, a local professor investigated and found the case to be entirely accurate. Dr. Ian Stevenson, the University of Virginia researcher who has devoted a lifetime to studying past-life memories, reinvestigated the claims in 1964 when the girl was ten and also found the memories to be accurate. Many of the details were very specific. For example, at one point she had been forced to sell her jewelry to support herself. Also, she knew the woman kept a cobra as a pet.

ROVING RESEARCHER

Dr. Stevenson has traveled to virtually every country in the world to study children who seem to have been born with past-life memories. Among the children he interviewed, these memories were recalled as soon as the child was able to talk, dimming by ages five to ten and then forgotten permanently.

Most of his cases are from cultures that believe in reincarnation, for example, India. And yet a credible collection of cases has occurred in the United States, Turkey, Europe, and Asia. In all, he has cataloged more than two thousand cases and has published dozens of scholarly papers and books, many of them by the University of Virginia Press.

One of his most famous cases was that of Chanti Devi, an Indian girl who lived in the 1930s. When she was seven, she began to speak of a past life in Delhi; her name had been Ludgi. She had been born in 1902, was married, had had three children, and had died of childbirth complications with her third child.

In 1935, the case came to a climax when a cousin of the girl's alleged past-life husband visited Chanti's house on business. The girl immediately recognized him and the startled man was able to verify much of the information. Ludgi's husband was still alive at the time, and, of course, wanted to meet the girl. He arrived unannounced at her home and did not identify himself. Chanti immediately recognized him. She then traveled to her former home and pointed out a well site that had been dug, but had been covered over.

The case was thoroughly investigated by the local authorities, including a commission of judges, attorneys, and citizens, and was felt to be authentic. The case of Chanti Devi became the gold standard for scientific research into past lives as well as another in a long list of cases that buttress belief in reincarnation.

NOW AND THEN

Most researchers have focused on attempting to verify the accuracy of past-life details. When these details are learned, they conclude that the cases, such as those cited above, are proof of reincarnation. Others, including Professor Charles Richet, one of France's leading physiologists and paranormal researchers, and Dr. Edwin Zolik, of Marquette University, have focused on the current lives of subjects and have frequently found the source of the past-life memories.

For example, one subject, who in a past-life memory could speak fluent Greek, was found to have a precise knowledge of the grammar found in a modern Greek-English dictionary. In another case, a subject reported that he had been thrown from a horse and killed in his past life. Further study found that his grandfather had died after being thrown from a horse. The grandfather's accident occurred when the subject was very young, but he no longer had a conscious memory of it.

Dr. Reima Kampman, a psychiatrist at the University of Oulu, Finland, began her research into past-life regression in the 1960s, studying two hundred students ages twelve to twenty-two.

She found that it was relatively easy to hypnotize her subjects to uncover past-life memories and that nearly half the students in her study had such memories. She then studied the characteristics of those students and found that they had better mental outlooks on life than those who could not recall past-life memories. She further asserted that they were less neurotic and could handle stress better.

Under hypnosis they would tell her the origins of their past-life memories. In virtually every case, her subjects could recall where they had gotten the information.

One dramatic case involved a nineteen-year-old girl who produced eight past lives, including one with a detailed description of a Nazi raid over Finland, others with the names of her parents, addresses, and so on. It turned out she had incorporated the information into her memory by chance from a book in the library. Under hypnosis, she was able to give the name of the book, the author, and even where the details were located in the book.

The case of Edward Ryall, as examined by Dr. Stevenson, is another example. Ryall lived a quiet life in Essex County, England. When he was about seventy, he suddenly began to be flooded with memories of another life, which occurred while he was conscious, not under hypnosis. He distinctly recalled being born in 1645 and being raised on a farm in England. His name was John Fletcher. His parents died when he was young, and by the time he was a teenager, he ran the family property. He eventually married, sired two sons, and died in the British Civil War of the 1680s.

The sheer details of his story, along with vivid descriptions of life in the seventeenth century, made this case convincing as an authentic past-life memory. But as Dr. Stevenson investigated further, he found many discrepancies in Ryall's story, for example, the incorrect use of Old English (the words were already archaic in the 1600s) and the layout of the landscape. Ultimately, the case was felt to be one of cryptamnesia, the unconscious gathering of material from reading and experience and which comes to consciousness. There have been many such cases during the past one hundred years in which professional mediums, psychics, or ordinary citizens have recalled detailed memories of past lives. These vivid details have come directly from either history books or novels.

How this occurs is unclear. Somehow, material from literature fragments into memories we think of as our personal history. For example, a child might read a story. Although the memory of that story is forgotten in the general consciousness, fragments from that mass of information are stored as personal memory.

TRULY UNEXPLAINED

Even so, many anecdotal cases of past-life memories cannot be resolved by invoking cryptamnesia. Often, the past-life memories contain information unknown to our society at the time of disclosure. Other times, inherent in the past-life memory is information that the person having the memory would not be able to access. This includes detailed information about the life and times of ordinary citizens that only scholars and historians are aware of and then only after extensive research.

For instance, there remains a pool of cases that include not only memories of people and places, but of their personal traits as well, which continue to confound experts. An example of this, again in India, involved a young boy who, by age five, could vividly describe numerous details of a past life. He was taken to his former home where, in addition to recognizing his family, he immediately began to play the drums with great skill. He had not previously displayed this skill, and the person he felt he was reincarnated from did play the drums.

What makes this account thought provoking is that skills and abilities such as playing drums involve different mechanisms and neurobiological pathways from those that store images and language. The ability to play the drums is often unconscious and involves complex interactions between the motor areas in the brain. One of these areas, by the way, is located in our right temporal lobe.

Stranger yet is Dr. Stevenson's assertion that even birthmarks can indicate the truth about a past-life memory. Stevenson has collected hundreds of stories in which a child remembers, for example, living a previous life and being killed by a gunshot wound to the head. That child at birth bore birthmarks that looked remarkably like a gunshot entry and exit wound.

Another confounding story is that of Victor Vincent, a fullblooded Alaskan Tlingit. Toward the end of his life, in 1946, he became very close to his niece. He predicted he would be reborn as her son and claimed she would know him by the birthmarks he would have. Vincent had a distinct surgical scar on his back and another at the base of his nose.

In December 1947, almost two years after Victor died, the niece gave birth to a son. The son, Corliss Chotkin, had two birthmarks that precisely matched his uncle's scars. When the baby was a year old, his first words were, "Don't you know me? I'm Vincent." The boy initially recalled many details of Vincent's life, but ultimately forgot them all by age nine.

My initial opinion was that this was a case of paramnesia, a phenomenon that occurs when a family's expectations create memories that are implanted in the child. Certainly, the infant must have grown up hearing about his late uncle's desire to be reincarnated as his niece's son. Such expectations can generate family myths that the child might unconsciously be acting out. However, paramnesia does not account for his being born with the same scars.

Fears and phobias also have been reported to have been transmitted as a facet of past-life memories. A case in point is that of a woman in Texas who reported that for years she had been obsessed with dreams of walking on the catwalk of a bridge and falling. These fears did not seem to be connected to her current life. One day, she picked up *Life* magazine and saw a picture of the bridge she had seen in her dreams.

She said, "The picture of the bridge was taken from the same angle from which I always approached in my dream. The article accompanying the picture identified it as the first cat-walk constructed across the East River preparatory to building the Brooklyn Bridge in the 1870s. It also stated that a number of persons, both men and women, had fallen to their deaths from the bridge. I am convinced I was one of those because, after reading the article, I have never had that particular dream again and the lifelong fear that I would die from falling from a great height has been dispelled."

Many reincarnation believers offer such cases as proof of past lives. Their argument is that since there is a real phobia or fear that can be documented, and the fear or phobia is cured as a result of the uncovering of the past-life memory, it must be a "real" past-life memory. Indeed, there is some research that can be seen to support this. We learned from false-memory research, for instance, that when *real* trauma occurs, phobias and fears frequently result. Conversely, when false memories are *implanted*, phobias and fears rarely ensue.

MEMORY CONVERGENCE

If there is a point of convergence for NDEs, cryptamnesia, past lives, reincarnation, false memory, and other anomalous phenomena involving memory, it is likely to be found in the right temporal lobe, probably anchored in the life review as experienced by the children I have studied. Rather than fixating on the validity of the life review, I firmly believe it is more valuable to accept the lessons it can offer.

The life review is a time for learning, for interaction with ourselves in a unique state of dual consciousness. During the typical life review, the person views important scenes from his or her own life and learns from them. For example, Dannion Brinkley, in the book *Saved by the Light*, describes how his life review included scenes of when he was a bully as a child and often beat up classmates for no reason other than the fact that he could do it. In the course of his life review, he felt the pain he had inflicted on others.

From our conventional understanding of how memory works, this would seem to be an embellishment Dannion added afterward. Although it is possible to suppose he remembered being a bully, conventional thinking would not permit him to "remember" someone else's pain.

Yet that is not what Dannion and others who have had life reviews as a result of NDEs describe. They state emphatically that they felt the physical and mental pain from the perspective of the victim. Further, they state that this experience caused them to grow spiritually and to be transformed. They actually tapped into the universal memory bank and felt the experiences of other people.

ACROSS THE BOARD

I believe that vivid memories can be imprinted in a particularly strong and pervasive way in the universal energy field. These memories then express themselves in unpredictable yet recognizable patterns. This explains the birthmark studies, in which people who claim to be reincarnated have birthmarks that correspond to the wounds of those from whom they are reincarnated.

Finally, we have a mechanism to understand what Dr. Stevenson calls the most compelling evidence of universal memory, these birthmark cases. These physical traits are encoded in the universal memory fields that are all around us, in the chairs we sit on, in the grass, in the clouds—they are hidden in the visual and auditory images we are constantly bombarded with.

Such fields or patterns are stored similarly within the developing fetus. As the fetus develops, embedded into the biological plan of the developing organism are genetic instructions to form such birthmarks. These birthmarks are genetically determined, encoded within the DNA that creates the pattern of developing life. So when someone dies a dramatic death—a drowning, for instance—he or she may have a fear of water in the next life.

Such patterns could easily express themselves in unpredictable ways, since the pattern exists in the subatomic reality that is not perceptible to our senses. After all, most of life goes on at a level that is imperceptible to us. In that sense, life may seem to be irrational, yet it occurs in very patterned ways.

No Coincidences

All of this still doesn't answer the question that I am asked so many times by patients: "Dr. Morse, do you believe in reincarnation?"

Given all the research, I would have to answer that question with a resounding "probably." Not only is it a common belief among all the world's peoples (including those in developed countries like the United States and Europe), but it is one that is backed up by excellent research. Dr. Stevenson's work, for instance, surpasses ordinary anecdotal research. In his work, he examines all of the minutiae of a case in great detail. He presents the case in a graph akin to a detailed family chart, recording all of the names of the people used to cross-check the information presented in the case. His evidence tables can go on for several pages, and are painstakingly detailed.

In reading the work of many other fine reincarnation

researchers, I arrive at the same conclusion that the late Carl Sagan did regarding this subject. "There are three claims in the ESP field which, in my opinion, deserve serious study," said the normally skeptical scientist. One of those is "that young children sometimes report details of a previous life which [are] accurate."

One such case is from the files of Dr. Stevenson. Parmod Sharma was born in 1944 to the family of a professor living in India. As Stevenson wrote:

> When he was about two and a half, he began to tell his mother not to cook because he had a wife in Moradabad who could cook. Later, between the ages of three and four, he began to refer to a large soda and biscuit shop which he said he had in Moradabad. He asked to go to Moradabad. He said he was one of the "Mohan Brothers." He claimed to be well-to-do and to have had another shop in Saharanpur. He showed an extraordinary interest in biscuits and shops . . . he related how in the previous life he had become ill after eating too much curd and said he had "died in the bathtub."

Stevenson interviewed the child at length and then questioned the family, learning that they had no previous knowledge or friendship with anyone named Mohan. Stevenson then found a biscuit shop in Moradabad known to be owned by the Mohan brothers, who owned another biscuit shop in Saharanpur. After interviewing the brothers, he discovered that they had a brother who had died of a gastrointestinal illness shortly after taking a therapeutic bath.

"Old" science would dismiss this case as some sort of "one in a billion" coincidence. These scientists would say that perhaps the young boy picked up the information at school or from a traveling family member even though Stevenson's painstaking research showed that no such exposure took place.

My medical school professor, mentioned earlier, used to lecture that to resort to coincidence as an explanation is the first refuge of the lazy mind. "Remember, when you invoke coincidence, you only have a one in a million chance of being right," he used to say.

I agree with him.

5

Angels and Ghosts in Nature

It SEEMS THAT EVERYONE HAS A GHOST STORY TO TELL. A house in which residents hear mysterious noises . . . A father who saw his son standing in a doorway when the boy was actually dying in Vietnam . . . A mother who meets a psychic who actually seems to be communicating with her dead son.

Even doctors aren't immune. When I interned at a San Francisco hospital, many of the doctors on overnight duty told of an elderly man in old-fashioned dress who "visited" many of the residents and interns. He was assumed to be one of the hospital's early doctors. To be visited by the "old man" was felt to signify that he approved of the young physician's skills. Every chief resident who had worked as an intern in the past thirty years at that hospital had been visited by this specter.

Angel and ghost sightings have many elements in common with NDEs, including the fact that the perception of them is mediated by the right temporal lobe.

People who have had NDEs are more likely to see ghosts and angels. Take the children who attended the near death picnic, for instance. One of the girls who had an NDE was visited for years by the being of light she had seen when she almost died. This angel would appear to her when she was under stress of any kind, be it fear or anxiety. The angel was always helpful and left her full of strength and positive feelings.

Now, at the age of twenty, this woman no longer sees her angel, yet feels that that light instilled in her the power to handle pretty much any crisis that might arise.

A MATTER OF PERCEPTION

On its most elemental level, our right temporal lobes are responsible for communicating with the universal mind, or what some people might call the holy spirit. Just as one area of the brain processes information from patterns of energy picked up by our ears, another processes information from patterns of energy interpreted by our eyes. The right temporal lobe picks up energy patterns and interprets them. These patterns seem to contain the code for spiritual experiences and communications with other realities.

Sometimes, however, these energy patterns can be mediated through other objects or living things, like the sudden operation of radios or music boxes. For example, a doctor in Toledo, Ohio, told me that a cactus in her house blooms faithfully each year on the anniversary of her daughter's death in March. To her, this is a sign that her daughter's life is renewed again.

I do not know how the Christmas cactus changed its blooming cycle. Was it the mother's grief forming such a powerful need that the universe responded to it? Was her daughter trying to send her a message that she was not able to receive through visions so she changed the pattern of energy that affects the plant's blooming cycle? I don't know the answer. I do know that the altered blooming cycle served to memorialize the love between this mother and daughter.

Just as it is difficult to explain visual images to someone who is blind, it is difficult to appreciate visual images that are not being received through our eyes. As a result, we think they must be hallucinations, but in fact they are perceptions of patterns of universal energy.

Ghosts, disembodied souls that appear in a bodily form, often seem to represent a sort of memory of traumatic events localized to a place. No fewer than seventeen ghosts, for example, are said to haunt the Tower of London, the site of many deaths throughout English history. Sightings of Abraham Lincoln's ghost in the White House is another example.

Hauntings, in fact, are similar to memories that are embedded in the area where they took place. The tragedy of a mother grieving for a child who has died, or a lovers' quarrel that results in death, are the sorts of events likely to be replayed again and again at the site of their occurrence. These embedded memories, or engrams, include a combination of emotion, visual and auditory images, smells, and tactile perceptions.

CLUES AND SENSATIONS

People who have sensitive right temporal lobes are more likely to see ghosts. These sightings are often accompanied by specific cues and sensations, like fragrant smells.

Dr. Vernon Neppe, a pioneer in the study of paranormal abilities, fell into a conversation with the lighthouse keeper of a lighthouse he was visiting on the Washington coast. They discussed the grounds, with the stark, wind-blown, twisted appearance of the trees and the hardy scrub grass that survives so close to the sea. The lighthouse keeper said, "You know, it's funny. Although I have never seen it, there is a fragrant flower around here. I smell it all the time."

Looking around, Dr. Neppe realized that no flowers grew

there and surmised that the lighthouse keeper was having right-temporal-lobe sensations, the type that usually precede hauntings. He then said casually, "So, tell me about the ghosts you have seen around here."

The lighthouse keeper turned pale and said, "How did you know? I have never told anyone about seeing the old mariner's ghost on rainy nights." A lucky guess? Perhaps. Virtually every old lighthouse has a ghost story. It is also true that old lighthouses have histories of dramatic death and deep emotion associated with them.

Studies of right-temporal-lobe sensitives show that they frequently have experiences associated with hauntings—hearing bells, having goose bumps and a prickly feeling at the back of the neck, déjà vu, out-of-body perceptions, sweating, sleep disturbances, partial amnesia, auditory perceptions of voices or music, feelings of numbness and tingling of the arms or legs, perceptions of whirling balls of lights and faces. These are perceptions that have been directly linked to right-temporal-lobe activity. It is my belief that most of these perceptions take place through the right temporal lobe's link to a universal memory bank.

COMMON GROUND

Here's a well-documented case from the 1950s, in England, that illustrates my point. Miss E. F. Smith, with her little dog, was driving home from a party near her home in Letham, a small village in the countryside. Her car skidded off the road and wasn't drivable. She put her dog on its leash and began walking home.

As she crested a hill, she saw figures carrying burning torches in a distant field. As she came closer, she noted that the men wore tights and short tunics and seemed to be searching the ground. Her dog began to growl and bark and had to be restrained, an indication that the figures were visible to him as well. One of the most curious aspects was that the figures seemed to be following a circuitous route, as if an invisible barrier prevented them from moving into certain areas. This incident is strikingly similar to stories of past-life regression or déjà vu with the exception that she was not being hypnotized, but actually saw it happening.

When she told her friends and neighbors about it, she was referred to investigators at the Society for Psychical Research, who found she was giving an accurate account of clothing and weapons from about A.D. 600. Furthermore, unknown to Smith, a brutal clash of English clans had occurred along the shores of a shallow lake that existed in A.D. 680. This important battle had resulted in the death of one of the clans' kings and a historic consolidation of power for the others. That lake, which had since dried up, corresponded to the invisible barrier.

As we have discussed, these engrams involve memory being embedded in an area in the form of visual, auditory, and emotional images, which this anecdote illustrates. They become, in essence, a part of universal memory.

Universal memory is best understood as a morphic field, the shape or pattern of energy underlying everything that we call reality. It's similar to the programming that lies at the heart of the operation of computer software.

When Smith looked over the fields of modern-day England, she initially saw trees, grass, sky, and stars. But Smith had a visual perception of a memory engram embedded in the countryside, like the person who taps into a past life or perceives a past memory as déjà vu. This engram was created by the powerful events that led to the original battle, the retellings of the battle, and the anguish of those whose loved ones died. That morphic field was shaped over time by this input and resulted in the scene Smith saw.

GHOSTS—A HISTORY LESSON

In the late 1800s, the most prominent scientists of the time came together to try to understand consciousness as it relates to the ability to leave the human body and survive death. They formed the prestigious Society for Psychical Research (SPR) in England. This organization and its American branch, the American Society of Psychical Research (ASPR), have dominated serious scientific research on the paranormal for years.

Their first subjects were ghosts and hauntings. In 1882, at Cambridge University, the SPR included physics professor Sir William Barrett; Henry Sidgwick, who was devoted to reconciling religion and science; his wife, Eleanor, a mathematician; and Frederick Meyers.

These investigators left behind a body of research never since equaled. Their greatest contribution was the *Phantasms of the Living*, a hefty tome in which they describe most ghostly apparitions as hallucinations generated by telepathic messages from people in deep emotional crisis. Here, they expose many frauds as well as present meticulously detailed cases for which they had no explanation. Ultimately, the SPR concluded that ghosts were not proof of spirits still on earth, but were, rather, memory still embedded in reality.

I have read more than ten thousand ghost stories and have spent many hours in the National Institute of Discovery Sciences library, reviewing the hundreds of volumes it has on consciousness research. My informal estimate is that the vast majority of ghostly hauntings involve places in which the memories and perceptions seem to reside in the environment.

One of the best examples is the World War II fighter-bomber *S Is for Sugar*, which was stored in London after the war. On occasion, phantom gunners in full flight dress have been observed manning the plane's turrets. Even when the plane was moved across town to a museum, the sightings continued at the new location. Real ghost busters refer to these sightings as "recurrent localized apparitions," meaning that something is seen repeatedly in the same place, and the images are seen by several people at the same time.

One of the SPR's best-documented cases was that of a ghostly woman, originally described by a Rosina Despard, a young medical student who saw the woman in her home. She stated, "I had gone up to my room when I heard a noise. Thinking it was my mother, I got up and went into the hall. In the passage, I saw a tall lady, dressed in black, standing at the head of the stairs. After a few moments, she descended the stairs. I followed at a short distance." Despard gave a detailed description of the woman, who had a white handkerchief in her hand and lace cuffs at her wrists.

Over the years, several others saw the same apparition. This was between 1880 and 1889. Some people saw the apparition during the day and mistook it for a real person. A guest, who knew nothing of the ghost, asked, "Who is that woman in the other room, and will she be joining us?"

The SPR closely investigated the case. They found that the family was of good character and reputation. The SPR also found that many people, including neighbors, guests, and casual visitors, saw the woman. The phenomenon was so familiar there was often little reaction after sightings. On one occasion, children formed a ring around the woman, who then disappeared.

The image did not seem real, but rather like a faded stain on cloth. Sometimes the apparition would be in a room, seen by some and not by others. Some only heard noises, while others felt a rustle of wind and faintly perceived someone as being present. Others saw the complete visual image of the woman, even in broad daylight and outdoors. Sightings occurred in daylight, at night, in the house, and in the yard. Infrequent by 1886, the sightings stopped altogether by 1889.

The family believed the apparition to be the second wife of a former owner of the house. Heavy drinkers, the couple quarreled frequently. The woman left the house and divorced her husband, who died soon after. She died a few years later. Despard saw a picture of the woman and identified her as the "ghost." What are we to make of this story and the thousands of similar ones that have been documented from those days to the present?

First of all, they clearly are not hallucinations, mass hypnosis, or psychosis. This story and many like it illustrate the fact that often people who have never heard of the particular ghost have seen it. Furthermore, the medical student saw this woman for two years before she spoke of her. During that time, at least three others also saw her and didn't talk about it. The experience has much in common with a three-dimensional memory engram in that noises, smells, and visceral sensations, as well as visual images, are part of the experience.

Once the initial sighting was made, there was an acceleration of sightings until the mystery was finally solved. Then the sightings didn't occur again. This is a common pattern in ghost stories and an excellent example of a haunting that is simply a memory, the memory of the woman and the house she lived in and loved.

Her presence was replayed over the years, a pattern of movement coupled with an intensity of emotion: anger, love, rage, etc. This pattern was stored as a morphic field.

Certain people who had well-tuned, sensitive right temporal lobes accessed this memory and saw it in three-dimensional form.

MEMORY IN THE MAZE

There is considerable experimental evidence supporting the existence of morphic fields.

Beginning at Harvard in the 1920s, William McDougall did studies on rats learning to run mazes. McDougall used standard laboratory rats and trained them in a water maze. After swimming through the maze, they came to two exits, one with a dim light, which would give them a shock, and one without a light, which was safe.

The first generation of rats took 165 tries to learn which was the best exit. Subsequent generations learned more quickly. By the thirteenth generation, it took only 20 tries to get it right. The rats were not teaching subsequent generations since they were raised in isolation from each other. Furthermore, the striking improvement was not due to breeding smarter and smarter rats. McDougall would deliberately use the least successful rats, who were the worst at running mazes in general. Yet the slow rats of subsequent generations could complete the water maze more quickly than the original rats.

McDougall assumed that inherited learning had taken place, that an evolution and modification of the rat genes had allowed the faster learning. But years later, when rats with no biological connection to McDougall's rats were tested in the same maze, they ran it properly after just twenty tries. Could it be that the maze contained memory, cues perceived by the modern rats' right temporal lobes that allowed them to benefit from the schooling of the early rats?

Charles Darwin, the father of the theory of evolution and random selection, described a case of embedded memory. He wrote about a dog that had been mistreated by a butcher. As a result, the dog had a violent fear of and aversion to butchers. This fear was transmitted through two generations of offspring. Even his children and grandchildren feared, and fled, whimpering, from butchers even though they had not been mistreated by them.

Examples like these are best explained as occurring through the same mechanisms that create ghostly hauntings. As the rats learn to run the maze, their memories are stored in nature itself, and are altered and improved as more runs occur. Future rat generations access that memory. The result is that they can run the maze faster as they benefit from the learning of prior generations.

CONSISTENT STORIES

My analysis of more than ten thousand ghost stories convinces me that they represent complex interactions between the individual and universal memory. We tap into this universal memory in the same way that a radio receives radio waves. And, just as the air around us is filled with radio and cell phone waves, it is also filled with thought and memory from people and events, both past and present. When tapping into this memory field, the right temporal lobe acts as a receiver because it is at times calibrated to receive memory that exists in the universal memory bank. This memory is usually perceived in the same way by all who tap into it, which is why there is such consistency among ghost stories.

One excellent example of this is a well-documented ghost story that took place in Turkey in the 1950s. Leon Weeks, an American archeologist, was working at an ancient site near Gallipoli. He had little knowledge of the war and no contacts in Australia or knowledge of Australian culture and history. He set up camp at the site of the famous battle of Gallipoli, in which thousands of Australians were slaughtered in a disastrous campaign.

One evening, he saw a man scrambling down a nearby hill, leading a donkey that appeared to have a human body draped over it. Weeks pursued the man, but he disappeared. Night after night, he saw the man and the donkey, yet he could never communicate with the man. He left the site without solving the mystery.

In 1968, he visited a good friend, an Englishman who had an extensive stamp collection. There, among the Australian commemoratives, was a stylized version of the scene he had observed at Gallipoli. This stamp, his friend explained, was issued in 1965, fifteen years after Weeks had worked in Turkey, to honor the heroism of Private John Kilpatrick, an English soldier who had served as a stretcher bearer on the battlefield. He and his donkey were a familiar sight as he risked his life to retrieve the dying and the wounded. He is credited with having saved hundreds of lives before being killed by shrapnel. Kilpatrick was buried in the rocks of Gallipoli.

PAST-LIFE GHOSTS

This experience is best understood within the modern scientific context of universal memory. The battle at Gallipoli was deeply emotional. The loss of life is acknowledged to have been unnecessary. Many Australians believed that their sons were used by the English as cannon fodder for a military strategy that was wrong. This is precisely the sort of tragic emotional event that results in a powerful memory engram.

Within the Australian unconscious, those memories, over time and retelling, coalesced into the heroic image of John Kilpatrick. Ultimately, that vision resulted in the artistic image depicted on a commemorative stamp. To someone with a sensitive right temporal lobe who was alone on the same battlefield on which the morphic field was created, that same refined image presented itself in three-dimensional form more than a decade before the stamp was made.

Remember, the energy fields that store universal memories

exist in a timeless, spaceless place. When we enter into the universal mind, time has no meaning, as evidenced here when Weeks entered the universal mind to envision an image that would not manifest itself as a commemorative stamp for more than ten years. The artist who created the stamp also envisioned the same image, but ten years later.

A problem with developing a coherent theory of ghost stories is that there are so many, and it's tempting to present stories that fit within my theory. I have made every effort to counter that by dissecting thousands of ghost stories and categorizing them. Repeatedly, well-documented ghost stories fall within a specific pattern:

- A localized haunting, meaning a haunted place as opposed to a ghost following a particular family or person.

- Some initial, deeply emotional event, usually involving love and/or tragic death.

- First one person sees the ghost, then others see or otherwise perceive it.

- The origins of the ghost are investigated and solved.

- The ghost disappears.

MODERN GHOST STORIES

Michael Norman and Beth Scott, who wrote *Historic Haunted America*, are professors of journalism at the University of Wisconsin. They interviewed eyewitnesses, spent nights in homes alleged to be haunted, and thoroughly documented sightings. I randomly selected one of the stories from their text to test my theory. I found interesting parallels.

They describe a haunting in the upper-middle-class suburb of Webster Grove, a well-manicured community in St. Louis.

In 1956, Mr. and Mrs. S. K. Furry bought the former Henry Gehm house on Plant Avenue. The Furrys had been married for twenty years and had two daughters. They were not psychics and had never had ghost experiences before.

One night, Mrs. Furry awoke and felt as though someone was in the room with her. She also felt an icy blast of air and then heard the sounds of a hammer striking the headboard of her bed. She heard the noises for several weeks and finally told her husband, a practical man, who thought it was simply the house settling, or her imagination.

One night, he saw a translucent shape and followed it as it drifted into his three-year-old daughter's room, where it vanished. Several weeks later, the daughter asked who the lady in black was who kept coming into her room at night. After nine years of such sightings, the Furrys sold the house and moved without telling anyone about the ghost.

A new family, the Whitcombs, moved in, a biochemist, his wife, and their two children. As we would expect from morphic resonances, even though they had heard nothing about ghosts or hauntings in the house, they immediately started to see ghosts. Like Mrs. Furry, Mrs. Whitcomb was awakened, this time by footsteps, and saw faint apparitions.

Unlike the Furrys, she was determined to learn the origin of the ghost. She researched the history of the home, going back to the original owners, the Gehm family. As she investigated, the manifestations increased in number and in character. Previously, there had been only ghostly apparitions and noises, but soon they also heard furniture moving.

One night, Mrs. Whitcomb felt a "message" to go to her mother's music box, which had been broken for many years. It suddenly worked perfectly. Later, she saw a sweater moving in the laundry room as if being thrown over a hanger by someone. She found herself saying aloud, "Mary Gehm, why did you do that?" even though, at that time, she had not learned Mrs. Gehm's first name. Another day, as if in a trance, she found herself going to the attic. Even though it had been thoroughly cleaned and straightened out by the Furrys, she found the furniture in disarray. In an open drawer, she saw blueprints bearing the Gehm name. She had been in the attic many times and had never seen the blueprints, but now they were in plain sight.

The family concluded that the Gehms, in some form, were still living in the home. As they came to that realization, the ghostly activities occurred almost daily, and were witnessed by the family and many friends. After solving the mystery of the ghosts, the Whitcombs moved out. The ghostly hauntings stopped in 1965 and have not recurred.

I do not believe a deceased family was trapped in the house. Rather, I believe the memories of a loving family, a father who built a house with his own hands, the daily patterns of living, the nightly trips to the bathroom, the joys and sorrows of family life, formed a memory engram that was trapped in the house. Once communication with the ghosts was established, they left the scene. It was as though the ghosts wanted to be found out so that a tension would be broken that would allow them to move on.

This is analogous to when I have trouble recalling the name of a movie star. Often, it will be a well-known personality, let's say Mel Gibson, whose name I know. But, for some reason, my memory is blocked. My efforts to retrieve the name become frantic. I ask my wife, "Who is the star of the Mad Max movies? You know, the handsome one?" I will remember everything about Gibson except his name. Then, as soon as I remember his name or someone tells me it, the psychic tension is relieved and I don't think anything more of it.

That is how I interpret the type of ghost stories exemplified by the Gehm house haunting. Such hauntings are a similar frantic communication between the universal mind and ourselves, a misplaced memory or psychic block that creates the same mental frustration and obsessive irritation that forgetting a known name or event can create in our minds.

Here's an example. After moving into a new house, a Boeing aircraft engineer visually encountered two ghosts. Sometimes they would be sitting and talking at the kitchen table. She found she could communicate with them telepathically and learned they thought they were still alive. When she informed them otherwise, they disappeared and never returned.

She then discovered that she seemed to have a gift for this sort of thing. "I have helped many spirits over to the other side," she says, including a spirit pacing back and forth on a sidewalk in downtown Seattle. "I used to think I was psychic, some sort of spiritualist, and I never felt comfortable with that. Now I know I can help the ghosts to the other side although I don't really even know what that means," she said. Perhaps she is simply attuned to the universal mind.

AFTER-DEATH VISITATIONS SIMILAR TO NDES

Between 50 and 75 percent of the population, when confronted with the loss of someone they love, will have an after-death communication from that person. Once again, simply from a lack of understanding, the mainstream scientific and medical communities dismiss these as hallucinations produced by grief and loss.

Our research team in Seattle was the first to document and suggest that such experiences are entirely normal, primarily because of their similarities to NDEs. If people can leave their bodies and go somewhere after they die, it seems credible that they can visit us after they die.

The hallmark of NDEs is that they involve dual realities, one vivid reality superimposed over another. The same vividly real flavor and sense of one reality being superimposed over this one is the hallmark of the after-death visitation and of parting visions in general.

Most of the communications are simple reassurances from those who have died. Yet there are more than enough cases in which new information was transmitted as part of the experience. This new information has even stood up in court, or has led to the solving of crimes. One of the most interesting of these cases involves a New England man whose son was murdered. After his son's funeral, he began to hear the son's voice in his head, telling him to go to a neighboring town. The father followed the directions given to him by his dead son. Finally, he located his son's car, being driven by his murderers. He blocked their car with his and called the police. Two men were arrested and convicted of the murder.

Those were the facts. Skeptics say the man was suffering from grief-induced hallucinations and coincidentally found his son's car. I am always amused when so-called men of science feel the need to believe in unlikely coincidences.

In theory, there doesn't seem to be anything controversial about communication with the dead. We have already documented the fact that such communication is possible and certainly occurs spontaneously. We know telepathy is a documented human function, so why is it controversial when people show strong proof that they have communicated with a departed spirit?

Although our physical bodies cannot exist in a nonphysical world, there is every reason to believe that consciousness or

memory can. Whenever I doubt the existence of a universal
memory bank, I think of cases I have encountered myself,
where ordinary people have extraordinary contact with the
other side.

In Vancouver, while counseling a group of parents whose
children had died of cancer, I heard a very convincing story of
after-death communications from one of the facilitators of the
group. She'd had an unusually vivid, recurring dream of a
small boy who seemed to be surrounded by soft, bright light.
A golden retriever ran to him and the two rolled around and
wrestled. This dream was so vivid that she had the perception
of being awake during it.

A few days after having had one of these dreams, she met a
new couple in the grief group whose son had died of cancer.
They mentioned that their son's dog had died several months
before his death and wondered if they were reunited in
heaven.

A puzzle was solved for the grief counselor. She told them
of her dream and learned that the son's dog had been a golden
retriever. There is no doubt that this dream had been meant
for this family.

The woman who had the dream had never had a psychic or
spiritual experience before. Although deeply religious, she is a
level-headed, commonsense sort who is deeply puzzled that
she would have had such a dream.

Another such event occurred in Seattle at Harborview Hospital. A teenage boy was killed in an accident while riding his
bike across the street. His mother was driving, a few cars back,
and came upon the accident. She rode with him in the ambu-
lance to Harborview and was with him when he died.

She returned home to tell her teenage daughter, who is
deaf, about her brother's death. She found her daughter in a
trance, communicating with her dead brother. The brother

told her the details of the accident, what heaven was like, and even the sex of their aunt's unborn child. He was happy, playful, and saying things to her like, "I know something you don't know," in a singsong voice.

She stayed in the trance for more than an hour while other family members gathered and communicated with the boy through her. Afterward, she revealed that she had come home from school and was watching television when her brother appeared and she fell into the trance.

Sometimes these mediumistic experiences can be facilitated through meditation. Stanford University psychologist Dr. Stanislav Grof does a type of spiritual meditation called "holotrophic mind therapy," which, in my opinion, is a training exercise for the right temporal lobe.

Many of Grof's patients have encounters with relatives and friends who have died. Though there is no way to verify independently that these patients are actually contacting the dead, the information gained is extremely convincing evidence of some kind of contact.

For example, one patient reported seeing the image of her dead husband. He greeted her and asked how she was doing. He was so vivid she found herself asking him questions about some legal papers regarding their estate, information that was essential and that only the dead husband knew about. Such an encounter might have been the tapping into of forgotten material in her unconscious mind and is not proof of true communication. However, the information came to her only after she had this vivid encounter with her dead husband.

Grof reports a more convincing case from a patient he calls Richard. During therapy, Richard experienced being in an eerie, luminescent space that was filled with discarnate beings desperately trying to communicate with him.

One of these messages was so concrete that Grof wrote it

down. Richard received a specific request to communicate with a couple in the Moravian town of Kromeriz. He was to let them know that their son, Ladislav, was all right. The message included a phone number and an address.

The communication puzzled both Richard and Grof, since it had nothing to do with the specific therapy being conducted at the time. After some hesitation, Grof telephoned the couple in Kromeriz and asked to speak with Ladislav. To his surprise, the woman began to cry, and said he was her son, who had died three weeks earlier.

UNIVERSAL COMMUNICATION

Years of hearing such stories has me convinced that spirits are not stuck between this world and another. Instead, we are in constant communication with the information contained in the universal memory. Some of these memories are so dominant that many people have access to them. Others act as a sort of psychic irritant. Sometimes the patterns of communication seem to come from specific individuals, while at other times it almost seems to come from a universal source most people call God.

When I encountered my first patient who'd had an NDE, I wondered, "How can a comatose brain process memories?" Now I know that many memories are embedded in the universal energy pattern and that we access them through our right temporal lobe. One of the children I studied summed it up nicely. When I asked him where he went during his NDE, he said, "I went out there where everything is. I could see everything and talk to everything because it's all around us all the time, we just can't see it most of the time."

When I think of what he said, it becomes easy to understand ghosts and angels.

6

Unraveling the Fabric
of the Universe

WHEN MR. DESCHAMPS WAS A BOY IN FRANCE, A DR. DE
Fortgibu gave him a piece of plum pudding. Ten
years later, he had occasion to have another plum
pudding, and it was the first time he'd had it since
he was a child. He was surprised to learn from his
waiter that a Dr. de Fortgibu had just been in the
restaurant and had ordered it as well.

He didn't have the opportunity to enjoy plum
pudding again until many years later. At a party, he
sat down to eat his pudding and remarked to his
friends that the only thing lacking was Dr. de Fortgibu. Suddenly, the apartment door opened and Dr.
de Fortgibu walked in. He was looking for a different party and had been given the wrong address,
which turned out to be the location of Mr. Deschamps's party.

It is difficult to dismiss this series of events as
mere flukes. Clearly, something more is at work
here, but what? With our study of the supernatural
in the previous chapter, we learned that ghosts, and

hauntings, are best understood as communications from and with the universal mind. We know that we are in constant contact with the universe, on an unconscious level, through the normal activities of our right temporal lobes.

In this chapter, we will learn that this communication is not restricted to loved ones who have died or heroic or tragic moments memorialized in time and space. The communication can result in interactions with physical aspects of the universe. Among these phenomena are remote viewing, telekinesis, and other powers from the margins of reality, including poltergeists and synchronicity, a type of universal intercommunication. The best way to visualize our proper relationship with the universe is once again to use a video-game metaphor.

There are, at least, two levels on which the game can be perceived: the actual images on the screen, and the binary code in the computer that puts the images on the screen.

For example, in a video game about tennis in which the figures on the screen hit the ball back and forth, there is, in fact, no ball at all, just a simple replicating pattern of zeros and ones—a binary code—which results from the movements of the controls and creates the movements of the ball.

Just as we perceive the quantum world as either an endless pattern of waveforms or visualizations of discrete particles, so it is with the video game. We can see the movement of the ball as either a part of an endless pattern of zeros and ones or as an object on a screen. The difference with human beings, of course, is that we are fully conscious characters on a three-dimensional video screen who are communicating, even altering, the underlying program.

CLEARLY HOLOGRAPHIC

The concepts that help us understand this come from the new scientific principles of quantum holography, a mathematical model of the universe in which every aspect of it, the entire universal pattern, is contained in every speck of matter.

The same is true in our bodies, where each cell contains all the DNA information necessary to create the entire body. For example, in each of our toes is everything the body knows about creating brain tissue. Every cell in the body holds the same DNA information. Beyond the DNA model, it also means that each of us has the means to gain access to an information bank containing specific information about virtually everything that was, is, and will exist in the universe.

Neurobiologists agree that the brain is holographic. To understand remote viewing, we need only to speculate that the holographic brain can communicate with the holographic universe. This isn't a great stretch, given that the brain is part of the universe.

The principle of the hologram is that every individual piece of matter contains all the information of the entirety. Since our brains are part of the universe, we have in each of us all the information of the universe—everything that ever was, is, and will be.

Dr. Raymond Moody, author of *Life After Life* and the acknowledged father of near death studies, once said to me, "Melvin, what if we are all just a three-dimensional video invented a thousand years from now?" Of course, he was joking (I think), but he captured perfectly the qualities of the holographic universe.

PARANORMAL NOW NORMAL

Quantum holography explains the phenomenon of remote viewing, the ability of humans to "see," with the mind, objects across time and space.

In ancient times, tribal shamans induced NDE-like experiences and left their bodies to look for animals to hunt. They also used the same state to accomplish physical and spiritual healing.

Psychologist Robert Moss described a shamanic experience he had that led to the healing of a woman named Wanda, a patient with breast cancer. "One night, in a dream state, I journeyed to check on her [his patient]. I found her in a night setting near a cave that was also a temple.

"She was frozen, paralyzed, in terror of some shadowy snakelike forms that menaced her. I grabbed two of the snakes and wove them into the form of a caduceus [the staff that represents medicine]. Instantly, the healing staff came brilliantly alight in my hand. It radiated intense gold light. I touched Wanda with it. She promptly vanished."

Wanda later told Moss that, on the same night, she dreamed a lucid dream in which he flooded her with light. This dream coincided with the dramatic improvement of her health.

Research documenting remote viewing is sound. It also has tremendous potential, as illustrated by Dr. Hal Putnoff's recently declassified work at Stanford University.

Putnoff did numerous studies for the Central Intelligence Agency (CIA) in San Francisco. There, test subjects were asked to focus on aerial photographs of cities to find an area that one of the test's administrators had selected. Putnoff found that people who claimed no psychic abilities at all were often skilled at locating these target areas. Other studies involved randomly selected college students who claimed no special psychic talents or even a belief in paranormal abilities. They too were quite accurate in their results.

For example, a merry-go-round was chosen as a target area and the choice kept secret from testers and test subject. The test subject was asked to concentrate and draw a picture of the target. In this case, monitors from the CIA acted as subjects. One agent described it, saying, "Some sort of structure, a rounded dome-like structure, with a thing on the top like an appendage, in the general sense a rounded top-style top. Perhaps a lightning rod on the top." He then drew a picture resembling a merry-go-round.

As a result of this sort of study, the CIA decided to explore remote viewing further. They asked subjects to scan a map of West Virginia and its rural mountains and tell researchers where certain objects were located. Test subjects were remarkably accurate in their remote scans. Even more exciting to the CIA was that the West Virginia/rural mountain studies were the first two trials of this kind, not simply examples of two successful trials in a string of unsuccessful ones.

In July 1974, subjects were asked to provide information on an important Soviet missile site. Again, this is not an example of the best-ever test result, but the very first result. The viewer, Pat Price, gave detailed drawings of a Soviet missile site in a remote area of the former Soviet Union. He "roamed" the facility and gave detailed remote-viewing information.

It is impossible to know how much of this information was used at the foreign policy level. The CIA was asked to analyze the ability of remote viewers to defeat the mobile MX missile system, in which missiles would have been shuttled from site to site in a complex "pea-under-the-shell" game to avoid targeting.

It was concluded that the Soviets also used remote viewing and could successfully identify both occupied and vacant sites.

The ultimate government study of remote viewing involved the *Discovery* space probe that flew past Jupiter. Joseph McMoneagle, a noted remote viewer who developed his talent after having an NDE, was asked to provide information on the planet prior to the data being received from the probe. His remote viewing provided precise information that was accurate when compared with information from the space probe.

INFORMATION PROCESSING

Remote viewing doesn't involve actually seeing something as much as it involves processing information through our right temporal lobe from the patterns of information contained in the universe.

Robert Jahn and Brenda Dunne of the Princeton University engineering department did a remote-viewing study involving more than three hundred trials with forty viewers. Their technique was to have a subject choose a place anywhere in the world as a target to visit in his mind for ten to fifteen minutes. The subject would choose his own place and his own time to be at the spot, and he would record details of the target location.

Their impressions were then compared with the notes of a person who would actually visit the target spot at the preselected time. In 14 percent of the trials, the observations of the two matched so completely that they were judged not to have been caused by chance or guesswork and were highly significant. Also, the distance of the target from the subject or the time of the viewing was irrelevant. This fits with our theory that remote viewing involves mentally tapping into a place that contains the information of the universe, one where past, present, and future have no meaning.

Everyone has the ability to practice remote viewing. Jeffrey Iverson, an investigative journalist for the BBC, told me he had a similar experience when he was researching a program on the remote-viewing laboratory of the American Society of Psychical Research (ASPR) in New York City.

Though ASPR researchers insisted it was a normal human faculty, Iverson doubted remote viewing. To prove it, the scientist asked his assistant, Tessa Cordle, to participate in a test. She was placed in a soundproof room. Then, researcher Dr. Nancy Sondow got in a car and drove around the city. She activated a random-number generator that selected a site as the target. She drove to the target and stayed for a while. At a predetermined time, they asked the subject, Tessa, to draw her impressions.

To her great surprise, Tessa suddenly "saw" an English park with a tarnished metal statue of an angel. She drew detailed pictures, which included a small nearby building, a street with shops, and a red-and-white-striped awning on the road alongside the park. Again, the actual description of the experience was right temporal in origin. She felt tranquility and quiet. She described what she saw as "a place people go to eat. You can think your own thoughts there. There is a place to eat and a deli."

She described the statue of an angel by saying, "It looks like a butterfly. There is something like wings, a long robe. There is a kind of metal that turns green. It could be a man. It's quite unobstructed. There are no buildings around it. You don't feel closed in. Maybe it was a recreational area at the turn of the century."

Her description matched the location that Dr. Sondow had driven to. I should point out that neither Cordle nor Sondow were ever thought to have any special psychic powers.

REMOTE VIEWING AND SYNCHRONICITY

The interconnectedness of life is real. This was one of Niels Bohr's first major concepts. The founding father of quantum physics discovered that an interconnectedness exists between apparently unrelated subatomic events.

Physicist Wolfgang Pauli and psychologist Carl Jung developed the concept of synchronicity before Bohr proved it existed. The theory is that hidden patterns in life can be expressed by seemingly coincidental events, and that these patterns represent communication with a conscious, universal mind.

Pauli was initially a patient of Jung. Soon they became partners in a search for inner harmony and symmetries in nature and the psyche. Jung traveled the world studying the dreams and myths of primitive peoples. He discovered that there are "archetypes," patterns that transcend individual cultures and into which we all can tap. In his study of the middle-class dreams of his fellow Viennese, he found images and patterns that also were found in the dreams of people in remote tribes in far-off lands. The result was a little like studying the languages of Western Europe and finding that most have a common origin in Latin.

Jung proclaimed that there was a common language of dreams and visions. The collective unconscious consists of material that has never attained consciousness in the "id," the individual's reservoir of psychic energy. The deeper levels of the mind belong to the entire human race, said Jung, rather than just a given individual. Jung believed that this collective unconscious not only had a language but also contained hidden meaning.

Jung had a patient with a highly rational approach to life, which was hindering her therapy. On one occasion, the woman told him of a dream in which a golden scarab, a beetle, appeared. The scarab was the Egyptian symbol for rebirth. The woman was puzzled by the bug dream. Just then, they heard a tapping on the window. A large beetle was trying to get in. When Jung opened the window, in it flew, a golden-green scarab, extremely rare in Vienna. When Jung showed the woman "her scarab," her excessive rationality was pierced, and she progressed in therapy.

Arnold Mandell continued Jung's work further, documenting not only that synchronicities have meaning, but that they occur at peak experiences, times of transformations, births, deaths, falling in love, psychotherapy, intense creative work, or even changes in profession. It was as if, Mandell stated, "this internal restructuring produces external resonances, or as if a burst of mental energy is propagated outward into the physical world."

UNIVERSAL EXPERIENCE FROM UNIVERSAL MIND

By looking at the nature of synchronicity, we can start to understand how it is related to ghost stories and past-life memories. For example, Zurich-based psychiatrist Carl Alfred Meier described the following story, which he felt represented a synchronistic event. An American woman, a surgeon at a mission hospital in the 1930s in Wuchang, China, was suffering from serious depression and traveled all the way from China to be treated by Meier. She told Meier of a dream that she had had, of the hospital with one of its wings destroyed. She was very involved with this hospital and felt that this dream of its destruction was the cause of her depression. He advised her to draw a detailed sketch of the crumbling hospital, which she did. Paradoxically, her depression immediately disappeared.

Many years later, the Japanese attacked Wuchang and bombed the hospital. The woman sent Meier a photograph of the destroyed hospital. It was identical to the drawing she had made years earlier.

We have now seen three versions of this sort of story in this book.

1. *Past life memories:* A woman had a recurring dream of falling off a bridge, which caused her depression. She saw a hypnotherapist and had a memory of falling from a bridge in a past life. She later saw a photograph in *Life* magazine of the exact bridge she had a past-life memory of, and learned from the photograph that this bridge, in fact, had collapsed many

years earlier and a woman had been killed. Her depression vanished after seeing the picture.

2. *Gallipoli ghost story.* In that event, an archeologist saw a ghost that exactly resembled a three-dimensional representation of a stamp which would be created ten years in the future.

3. *Synchronicity story.* The woman dreamed of a hospital that had been bombed, and the dream caused her depression. The woman drew a picture of what she saw in her dream, which cured her depression. Years later, the hospital was bombed in the war; she sent a published photo of the damage, which matched her drawing, to her psychologist.

Although these events are different, they all represent a communication with a universal mind, a pattern of events hidden in nature. Each person who experienced the pattern defined it for him– or herself in a different way, as a past-life memory, a synchronistic dream, or as a ghost story. Yet they are really all the same thing; in each case, a traumatic event emerges as a mental event. Those who have powerfully tuned right temporal lobes can access these patterns.

ON THE BALL

The work of Jahn and Dunne documents that all human beings have the ability to harness their psychic energy and project it into the physical world. In their laboratory, they built a machine that generates a cascade of falling balls through a random arrangement of pins, resulting in a randomly generated bell-shaped curve. The apparatus is ten feet high, six feet wide, and contains nine thousand polystyrene balls. These trickle downward from an entrance funnel onto an array of nylon pegs. The front of the chamber is transparent

Plexiglas so that the cascade of balls and their developing distribution is visible. Jahn and Dunne found that humans, simply by the power of thought, can significantly influence the cascade of the balls.

Some operators used formal meditation or visualization. Others attempted to identify with the machine and actually "be" the cascade of balls. Some used competitive approaches such as trying to outperform other operators. Many verbally exhorted the balls to change their pathways, pleading and/or threatening the inanimate objects. What was clear was that no one technique worked better than any other. And yet, they all worked.

What are the implications of these findings for the person on the street? They mean that we have to be careful about what we visualize and imagine. If by simply visualizing and using our imagination we can influence the movement of foam balls through a maze, it is logical that we can also alter other things unconsciously through the power of our minds.

WORLD AND CONSCIOUSNESS LINKED

The study of memory reveals that we are in constant communication with a universal energy pattern outside the body. We learn from the study of ghosts and synchronicity that we can receive communications from this universal energy pattern. We learn from remote viewing that when we try, we can access information from it. Finally, from the ball experiments we know we can actually alter reality in a physical way by interacting with that universe.

The astrophysicist James Jeans summed it up nicely when he said, "The concepts which now prove to be fundamental to our understanding of nature seem, to my mind, to be structures of pure thought. The pictures begin to look more like a great thought than like a great machine." What we call reality and what we call consciousness cannot be separated.

In essence, each thought we have is like a pebble being thrown into the subatomic environment—it spreads throughout all reality.

This explains many aspects of synchronicity.

For example, when Mickey Mantle died, there was a ceremony for him at Yankee Stadium. The number he wore, 7, was honored. The winning lottery number that day was 777.

There are no coincidences.

HEDGING BETS

Lottery numbers are chosen by the random selection of Ping-Pong balls falling through a mechanical device. Could it be that so many people that day were thinking the number 7 that their thoughts influenced the movement of the Ping-Pong balls in the machine? Is it more than a simple mechanical effect? Is it also universal communication?

We are all subtly influenced by others in predictable, measurable ways, which can be explained by the ball experiments. If we look at the movement of just one ball, we cannot see any effect from the human operator. If we look at the movement of thousands of balls over time, can we document the effects of conscious thought on reality? Consciousness ripples throughout reality like a pebble in a pond.

If the human mind can enter another reality the way people who have NDEs do, then it is certainly capable of determining such things as a sequence of randomly selected numbers. The question then becomes, Why hasn't someone figured out a way to profit from this? How come people continue to lose money at the craps and roulette tables in Las Vegas?

Gambling isn't a good example for two reasons. One, there are just as many players negatively affecting the movement of the dice as there are players positively affecting it. At the craps table, for instance, two players might cancel each other out.

Second, these are very subtle effects, only seen after thousands of runs. In Jahn and Dunne's ball studies, the results could be shifted only slightly. An extremely radical shift, where all the balls went one way or the other, never happened.

Each human mind seems to have only a small effect on the universal pattern. Each mind is only a small pebble in a huge lake, one in which many other pebbles are dropping and creating patterns.

ENERGY IN ACTION

I now have to share with you something that happened to us when our daughter turned thirteen. She was a troubled teen largely because, like all adolescents, her hormones went crazy. It seemed she was angry and screaming about something almost every night.

One evening, I was sitting at the dining room table when a dish came flying off the kitchen counter and nearly hit me in the head. I immediately looked at my daughter, thinking she had thrown it, but she was still at the other end of the table and at the wrong angle to have thrown the dish. We got up and looked around the kitchen and found that several of the dishes were broken; some were smashed to pieces inside the cabinets. We thought we had ghosts.

Then my daughter said something that cracked us all up and helped to resolve the problem. "I didn't throw that dish at you, Dad, but you make me so mad, I wish I had thrown it."

After that, things began to improve for her. There was never another flying-dish incident. I have wondered if there can be spontaneous mental destruction of dishes or other objects. There is plenty of evidence to show that we can serve as conduits of energy from a source outside our body, funneling and channeling energy to influence our surroundings. When that occurs, we call it poltergeist activity.

Poltergeists are known as "noisy ghosts," but are not really ghosts at all. Unlike ghosts, which are often localized to a specific place, poltergeists are localized to a specific person, usually a teenager going through puberty and experiencing rapid growth and a struggle with sexual tensions.

A well-documented case comes from a law firm in Germany, where in November 1967, Anne Marie Schneider was a teenage employee. Ever since the young girl had been hired, lightbulbs had been exploding, telephone bills had soared, calls were constantly disrupted, photocopiers malfunctioned, and power surged in the building, blowing out much of the equipment.

This case was investigated thoroughly by Professor Hans Bender of the University of Freiburg, and physicists Franz Karger and G. Zicha from the Max Planck Institute for Plasma Physics. Since the law firm suffered substantial financial losses, the Rosenheim Police Criminal Investigation Division took charge of the investigation.

They attached recording devices to the phones and showed, for example, that forty-six calls were logged during fifteen days, even though no one was actually placing the calls. Monitoring equipment documented the power surges, which typically coincided with the movement of objects and the explosions of lightbulbs.

By early December, events were happening virtually every hour. Power company engineers, police officers, and physicists watched as decorative plating left the walls, paintings swayed and moved, lightbulbs exploded, and file drawers were ejected from their cabinets. Twice, a file cabinet weighing more than four hundred pounds moved away from the wall on its own.

Anne Marie herself became more agitated during these events. It became clear to the investigators that these incidents were happening only when she was in the building. On several occasions, paintings were videotaped rotating on the walls, coinciding with the contractions of Anne Marie's arms and legs. When she was sent away, the disturbances stopped. After she found other employment, there were a few episodes at the new job. Then, not surprisingly, they ceased. Like the hauntings that they resemble, poltergeist experiences often stop when the person from whom they are emanating is discovered. It is as though the sudden focus on their powers interferes with their abilities to use them.

PREDICTING THE FUTURE

But could people be taught to use these abilities if they were asked to focus on them? If, say, schools taught students how to use the powers of the mind in the same way they teach the use of math and science, would there be any practical value? If teaching math has led to computers and space travel, what would teaching the mind to alter matter do? It is impossible to say, but there are excellent experimental studies documenting that humans have psychic abilities of all kinds that might be honed if people were led to work on them.

In one such study that I was involved in, entitled "The Impact of Premonitions of SIDS on Grieving and Healing," we documented that nearly 25 percent of parents who have had a child die of sudden infant death syndrome (SIDS) had a vivid premonition of that event. The hard data to prove this include journal entries and statements from physicians that the parents took their child to be examined shortly before the death occurred. Their pre-death sensations included dreams, feelings, or vague sensations of unease. Seven of the thirty-eight cases examined had only one sensation, which was described as either a visual or an auditory experience.

Could parents be encouraged to rely on their feelings as much as their rationality to watch over the health of their children? Many of the SIDS parents felt that comprehensive testing could have prevented their child's death. Based on the data from the SIDS study, I agree with them. The study found that premonitions of death were a common occurrence among SIDS parents and an uncommon occurrence among the control group. The difference between these two groups was quite large. Nearly 22 percent of SIDS parents had frequent premonitions of their children's deaths while less than 3 percent of the control group had a sense that "something" was going to happen to their child.

In addition to the nearly 25 percent of parents who had a premonition of their child's death, there were a number of parents who sensed that something life-threatening was wrong with their infant and sought medical care. This included children who had prolonged apnea, a phenomenon in which someone stops breathing for long periods of time.

Given the mysterious nature of SIDS, a problem with no known diagnosis, it is possible that even careful medical examination of these children would not have prevented their deaths. I have a tragic story from my own practice to illustrate this point. When I was in my residency training, a woman came to me with her infant daughter. The baby seemed to be healthy despite the mother's insistence to the contrary.

"I want you to check her out," the mother said. "I know my daughter is going to die."

I immediately examined the baby and even took a chest X ray to make sure that her lungs were clear of infection. I could find nothing wrong with the little girl.

"I want another doctor to look at her," she insisted. "I know there is something wrong with her."

I asked another doctor to examine the little girl and he too gave her a clean bill of health. The mother was very upset by our findings. I probed further. No, she had not had a recent death in the family nor had she had any kind of dream. "I am certain she is going to die," she said. "I can sense it."

The mother asked me to admit the baby to the hospital for one night, but given that I could find nothing wrong with her, I refused.

"Come back in a few days and let me take a look at her again," I said.

I will never forget the woman's eyes as she looked back at me. They were frightened and sad at the same time. "I hope she is alive in a few days," she said in a loud, clear voice that drew the attention of those in the waiting room.

To my great surprise, the little girl died the next night of SIDS.

I have often wondered what this woman perceived in her daughter. Were there physical clues from the baby that led the mother to a subconscious conclusion that the girl was in danger? Or did the mother connect with a universal source of information that told her the future?

Whatever the answer to those questions, it is clear that we must learn to take premonitions seriously, both ours and those of others. Whether premonitions represent contact with a universal mind or something indefinable that is deep within ourselves, they are a valid voice that should be listened to.

7

The Shape of Things to Come

ONE OF THE MOST INSPIRING CASES OF SPIRITUAL HEALING
I have ever encountered happened to an infant
patient of mine named Teryn Hedlund. By four
months of age, Teryn was dying of Wolman's disease, a usually fatal liver disorder caused by a
genetic defect in the way the body processes food.
Instead of being able to break down fats properly,
the body stores them in the liver, usually damaging
it beyond repair.

I diagnosed her with the disease in November
1993, but was waiting for the results of biopsy spec-
imens that had been sent to specialists at Pittsburgh
Children's Hospital and Portland Shriner's Hospital.
She was also thoroughly studied by metabolic and
liver specialists at Seattle Children's Hospital. All
agreed she was going to die.

I received her biopsy results the weekend before
Christmas. That weekend was the most difficult in

my career as a physician. Should I tell the family the day
before Christmas that their child was going to die, or should I
meet with them after Christmas, letting them enjoy the holi-
days together? Finally, I knew my job as a doctor was to give
them the facts, not to try to shield them. I told them that
Teryn would probably die soon.

But Teryn lived. Not only did she survive the crisis, she
went on to regain her complete health. For the first year, the
parents and I avoided discussion of her fatal diagnosis. Even
though she was growing and developing normally, I was reluctant to say anything about the case other than, "Well, she sure
is doing well. Let's keep a close eye on her." After a year went
by, we repeated her liver biopsy and found no trace of the disease. She was, in fact, cured.

Finally, a year and a half later, her mother got up the
courage to tell me how she thought the healing had taken
place. She said that her brother-in-law had cured Teryn the
same day I had given them the bad news.

I personally interviewed the brother-in-law. He did not look
like the typical spiritual healer. He told his story shyly and gave
the appearance of hardly believing it himself. He described
himself as a man who was not particularly spiritual or religious,
yet the night of the fatal diagnosis, he had heard a voice telling
him to put his hands on Teryn's abdomen immediately. To wait
until the next day, said the voice, would be too late.

The brother-in-law got up from bed and went straight to
Teryn's house. Without telling Teryn's parents why, he went to
her room and put his hands on the infant's abdomen, even
though he felt ridiculous. He felt warmth and saw a faint glow
emanate from his fingers; he never discussed it with anyone
until Mrs. Hedlund asked him what he had done. From that
very night, Teryn clinically improved.

To add to the mystery, Mrs. Hedlund reported another unusual experience surrounding the healing. Missionaries came to her door several weeks after Christmas and told Mrs. Hedlund they had a specific message to visit her. After being in the home for a few minutes and meeting Teryn, one missionary suddenly said, "I'm sorry, there has been some sort of mistake. It isn't necessary that we come here after all," and then left abruptly.

What is unique about this experience is that it was spontaneous and idiosyncratic, a pure gift from heaven to earth that appeared of its own accord. The brother-in-law does not consider himself a healer, and has not had spiritual experiences before or since this one. He is not starting his own church. Even though he experienced this, he has a hard time relating to it. He says, "Why would such a thing happen to me? Why would I be asked to heal Teryn?"

But really, why not? Like after-death communications, it came spontaneously and had a logic of its own that no one could have anticipated.

SEARCHING FOR CURES

These very odd and spontaneous aspects of Teryn's experience are the reasons the healing is so authentic. The everyday miracles I encounter have this flavor. They are rarely anticipated. Praying for them or directly asking for them doesn't seem to be a factor in their appearance, although, as we will see, there is ample evidence that prayers do have a positive effect on healing. We can only wonder how many times such events occur with the healing message not being heeded. How many times does a brother-in-law not follow through and complete the healing, or fail to act on an intuition?

As one mother who had a son die of cancer told me, "Dr. Morse, if it was just that simple—praying real hard to cure cancer—there wouldn't be so many like Justin [her son] and others dying." There isn't a mother I know who hasn't prayed her heart out to God for a miracle. I have been involved in many cancer deaths, and I know firsthand that every parent prays for a miracle.

What does Teryn's healing experience have in common with an NDE? As we will see, the common aspect of this healing, and spiritual healings in general, is the interaction with a mystical light, the same light seen during NDEs. Like the NDE, there is the perception of another reality intruding into this one—the voice the brother-in-law heard and the mystical light that appeared to come from his fingers as he massaged Teryn's abdomen. It was as though this flash of mystical light reconfigured her body's DNA, instantly reversing a potentially fatal genetic defect.

As we will see, scientific evidence indicates that having a dissociative experience (the scientific word for spiritual, out-of-body experiences and for NDEs) seems to be a common thread in healing.

SUDDENLY NORMAL

One dramatic example was reported by doctors at Duke University. They had treated an eight-year-old boy who had a severe genetic defect, one that is universally fatal by the teenage years. One day, as the boy neared death in his teens, all the cells in his body suddenly became normal. The genetic code was suddenly fixed.

It seems inconceivable that this could have occurred on the cellular level. It would have involved the precise and spontaneous mutation of millions of cells, all reverting to normal. This sort of case can only be understood as the sudden "healing" of the primary morphic form that made up the body.

"Morphic form" refers to a pattern of energy that gives

shape and form to what we consider to be reality, the actual shape of someone's body, for instance, or the form of a tree or a crystal. This morphic form is why we look like humans, and why dogs look like dogs, and so on. We all have a pattern by which we are created that exists from our earliest genetic inception.

This morphic form determines virtually everything about us, including hair and eye color, skin color, weight, height—the list is endless. Our morphic form makes us what we are almost from the moment of conception.

These morphic forms are not cast in stone. Sometimes, they can be changed through diligent effort. People who are born to be overweight can, and often do, become thin by carefully watching what they eat. Or, people who come from a long line of substance abusers and are "born" to be alcoholics often make conscious decisions not to drink at all. They are changing their morphic form, their destiny.

Mystical experiences have also been shown to alter the morphic form. NDEs are just such an example of this type of experience. Unlike the subtle changes that take place in a morphic field through the constant repetition of a new behavior, NDEs provide a powerful pulse of healing energy that immediately heals the morphic form.

When we review the scientific literature on miraculous healing, one important commonality emerges: Almost all involve right-temporal-lobe functions like out-of-body experiences, experiences of light, visions, and, of course, NDEs.

Most of these studies are useful in that they teach us what we can do to maximize our health, primarily by means of simple, inexpensive interventions, such as meditation or prayer, in our lives. They also clearly demonstrate that the mind has a powerful influence over the body, especially when communicating with God, or the universe, through prayer or meditation.

A HEALING GOD

Virtually all the anecdotal research or even controlled scientific studies stress that there must be an interaction between the mind of the individual and the universal pattern, or God. To carry this thinking further, I think NDEs unlock the secrets of how our minds can heal our bodies and how we can use our minds to maximize health.

An example of the power of this interaction is the often quoted Dr. Randolph Byrd study on the effect of prayer on recovery from heart attacks. In this study, parishioners in a mainstream San Francisco Christian church were asked to pray for 393 specific patients recovering from heart attacks. The people who prayed were not aware of the identity of those they prayed for. They prayed for that person from a distance. Concurrently, the subjects did not know whether or not they were being prayed for, nor did the researchers.

The study found that those prayed for by others recovered approximately 10 percent faster and better than those who were not prayed for.

The Byrd study was greeted with extreme skepticism by the medical community, where many felt the data were either wrong or had been misconstrued. The study was repeated several years later at Kansas City's Mid-America Heart Institute, using the same procedure and 990 heart patients. The patients prayed for in the Kansas City study did 11 percent better than the patients not prayed for.

William Harris, Ph.D., one of the study's investigators, seemed baffled yet pleased by the results. When asked to sum up the study, he just shrugged and offered this assessment: "The patients who were prayed for just did better. I mean everything that word means."

What can we learn from these studies? First, the act of praying matters. Second, the effect is fairly subtle. There were equal numbers of deaths in both groups in both studies, but those who were prayed for went home from the hospital about 10 percent sooner than those who were not.

Still, these studies lead to other questions that someday should also be subject to studies: Does on-site prayer work better than anonymous prayer at home? Does prayer from strangers work better or worse than prayer from loved ones? Clearly, more amplification is needed.

Nevertheless, these studies suggest the possibility that there is a universal energy pattern or collective mind that can directly influence health. These results could be predicted from our theory that those who are praying are contributing their healing energy to a universal pattern, subtly altering it so that there is a more rapid return of the healing body to a healthy morphic form.

DISSECTING PRAYER

The Spindrift Research Group in Oregon found that rye seed that was prayed over germinated more quickly than seed that was not prayed over. They then explored whether asking for a specific end result in a prayer was better or worse than simply asking for God's will to be done. They concluded that the most effective prayers were the ones that merely asked for God's presence.

Here's what the Spindrift Research Group had to say about the workings of prayer: "Scientifically, it is shocking to think of a force as intelligent, loving, kind, good and aware of needs. But each test prayer somehow linked to a loving intelligence moved the seeds towards their norms."

Their findings, that a nondirected approach to prayer works best, fits with my theory that prayer can bring an organism into closer harmony with its universal pattern.

THE FORCE THAT IS WITH US

Their theory is in harmony with the science of the twenty-first century. Biologists, astrophysicists, and mathematicians are already coming to a similar conclusion about the fundamental force behind the universe. Objective review of all of the data suggests that there is a spiritual force that is ever present in our lives, and that communication with that force is physically healthy for us.

For example, Leanna Standish has done some fascinating studies on homeopathic remedies in the treatment of AIDS. She is a Ph.D. psychopharmacologist who spent two years as a visiting scientist/fellow at the University of Washington's department of physiology and biophysics. She decided to study acupuncture and homeopathy in order to understand the healing power of the human mind. As she progressed in her studies of the primate brain, she began to believe that the function of the nervous system could not be explained by biology alone. She explored the concept of an alternative system involving energy fields that extend some four to six inches from the body.

She became research director of the John Bastyr Naturopathic College in Seattle, where she found herself in charge of a study of thirty HIV-positive males receiving alternative treatment. They received a combination of botanical medicines, homeopathy, psychological counseling, Chinese medicine, hydrotherapy, and artificial fever therapy, in which fever is induced to kill viruses. Their results were promising since they had higher survival rates than would be expected and fewer deaths than the norm.

She then developed specific homeopathic remedies for AIDS by using growth factors and cytokines (molecules that the brain uses to communicate with the blood), sending signals to the body to increase production of specific disease-fighting agents in the immune system, including interferon, tumor necrosis factor, and macrophage colony–stimulating factor.

It makes sense from a traditional medical viewpoint to inject factors into the body that will boost the immune system. Dr. Standish made incredibly dilute solutions of the factors, dilutions so weak that, in theory, there were almost no more actual molecules in the water. They were so dilute that skeptics of homeopathy scoffed and laughed, saying the treatments were simply make-believe treatments of water.

AIDS is not the sort of disease that responds to make-believe treatments of water. It takes "real medicine" to fight this horrible virus, and Dr. Standish's treatments turned out to be real medicine. In a double-blind, placebo-controlled study, the AIDS patients' immune systems improved. Blood-clotting factors increased, viral load went down, and, most important, patients gained weight and lived longer.

How could such a thing happen? Dr. Standish was puzzled but delighted.

"The implications are huge," she said. "What this might mean is that you can have a biological effect with no molecules [as in the prayer studies]."

How could something like this work? To me, the logical progression is as follows:

1. Nonmaterial forces, such as the force of the mind, have been proved to effect biological healing.

2. It is logical to assume that these nonmaterial forces work through some sort of universal energy pattern, one that forms the underpinnings of material reality.

3. This universal energy pattern (some call it God) responds by correcting errors in the localized pattern of energy which underlies a given human being.

WARTS AND ALL

For example, it has been documented that by using the power of the imagination warts can literally melt away. Numerous clinical studies, primarily with children, have shown that with a few hypnotic sessions, warts will disappear. The children are often instructed to imagine spaceships shooting lasers at the warts or God wishing them away.

I have seen this firsthand in my own medical practice. One patient, a Mormon girl, wanted to get rid of a number of warts that had grown on her hands. Medications and visits to a der matologist had been ineffective, so I suggested that she pray to God for their removal. Within weeks, all of the warts were gone.

A similar event happened with another patient. She had two warts on her stomach, but for reasons known only to children decided that she wanted to keep one and get rid of the other. As an experiment, I had her shoot the offending wart with imaginary laser beams while leaving the preferred wart alone. As you can guess by now, the target wart disappeared.

Medical science has no idea why this occurs. If we did, the fight against cancer would be greatly enhanced, as warts are tumors, albeit benign ones, growing in response to the stimulus of a virus.

This reminds me of an old pediatrician who first introduced me to the use of hypnosis in removing warts. He would carry a "wart stone" in his pocket. When he saw a child with a wart, he would take it out and give it to the child, telling him to rub it against the wart until the wart disappeared. The typical rate of spontaneous remission of warts is nine months. This doctor saw warts disappear with the wart stone generally within a week.

Here's an even better example of mind over body that's much more dramatic than warts, the case of Mr. Wright. His experience was reported in medical literature in the 1950s. Dying of lymphosarcoma, he had huge tumor masses throughout his body. A new anticancer drug, Krebiozen, came out and newspapers hailed it as an exciting advance in cancer treatment. Mr. Wright begged his physician to be put on the new drug, certain it would cure him.

Unfortunately, he did not qualify to get the new drug, since it was experimental and only a dozen patients were being treated with it. He begged for it, however, and was given the drug "off study."

Within three days of being given the drug, his tumors shrank to half their size. Soon he was strolling around the ward, joking and laughing. Within two months he had no evidence of tumors.

Unfortunately, the study patients did not do as well. They all died. This hit the newspapers and it was widely reported that the new miracle drug was a bust. Mr. Wright read those reports, and shortly thereafter relapsed.

At this point, his physician, Dr. West, the author of this case report, had an audacious idea. He wrote, "Deliberately lying to him [Mr. Wright], I told him a new, refined, double-strength version had just arrived." He even put off using the new version, which was simply water, until the next day to build Mr. Wright's anticipation. When he received water injections that he thought were the new version, his tumors melted away. The fluid in his lungs disappeared and he appeared to be in perfect health.

Unfortunately for Mr. Wright, just two months later a formal AMA report was widely distributed, saying Krebiozen was worthless. He again relapsed, and this time he died.

All physicians know that there is something called a "placebo effect," and that placebos, something like worthless sugar pills, which the patient believes to be "real" medicine, do actually heal the body. The question is: How do placebos work? And what exactly is the mind-body connection? This is truly a medical mystery.

PLACEBO THEORY

Now we can begin to understand the placebo effect. I propose a specific theory of how mind-body interactions take place. Furthermore, I link it to other energy-body interactions such as homeopathy, acupuncture, or Chinese *qi* medicine. All are proven entities. Now we must unravel this mystery and start to learn how to unlock the healing power of the mind.

The starting place, oddly enough, is with the stories that children tell after nearly dying, the NDEs. Typical of these stories is one of a child I will call Alice.

Critically ill from cancer, this ten-year-old was undergoing several rounds of chemotherapy. Her disease was quite advanced, and the doctors who treated her had been open with the parents in telling them that there was little hope of her recovery. Still, of course, everyone wanted to try and save her.

During one of her chemotherapy rounds, she was overdosed and nearly died from the medication that was supposed to be saving her. She was in a coma for several hours, but when she came out of it, she seemed very happy that everything had happened the way it had.

The story she told was typical of those who experience dramatic remissions. She claimed to have left her body and ventured into a bright light. In the light, there were friendly people, but one of them stood out in particular. It was a pleasant man with a beard who Alice described as "looking like Jesus."

"He told me that it was not my time and I had to go back and live in my body," she said.

From that point on, Alice experienced a dramatic remission of her disease. Her cancer came under control, and she has continued to make healthy progress.

Stories like this indicate to me that some patients receive help from beyond modern medicine. I know this may seem like a leap to some people, but a miraculous recovery after an NDE and an out-of-body encounter with a divine being tell me that, in this case, medical doctors aren't the only ones doing the healing. Somehow, perhaps through the biological connection of our right temporal lobe, we can receive help from a universal source of healing energy.

I am not the first to suggest such a connection.

The late Dr. Lewis Thomas was a well-respected physician/medical writer, as well as being the president of the Sloan-Kettering Cancer Center in New York City. He had flights of mysticism in his writings, especially when something unexplained took place in the world of medical science. Take the wart research, for example. When he read research showing that hypnosis could eliminate warts, he credited a higher being. "There almost has to be a person in charge, running matters of meticulous detail beyond anyone's comprehension, a skilled engineer and manager, a chief executive officer, the head of the whole place. But so far, whatever or whoever is responsible eludes comprehension."

Virtually everyone who has studied the healing power of the mind reaches a similar conclusion. Yujiro Ikemi, one of the foremost modern researchers of spontaneous healings (the type of healings nonmedical people call miraculous), proposes the following model: "All levels of organization are linked to one another in a hierarchical relationship so that a change in one necessitates a change in others." I would agree. I believe it is our right temporal lobe that creates changes within the body's immune system, and changes organization at the subatomic as well as the universal level of energy.

Here is another story to illustrate my point.

Rita Klaus had a complete, spontaneous recovery from multiple sclerosis. Remissions from MS occur, but she had a complete reversal of what had been thought to be permanent areas of damage.

On the day prior to her recovery, she was waiting for her husband to finish watching the eleven o'clock news. Suddenly, she heard a "very sweet voice that was inside me, outside me, all around me. I heard it say, 'Why don't you ask?'"

She was dumbfounded. She was very religious, and had prayed regularly but had not asked to be healed of her disease. She had felt bitter toward God and did not believe that he would heal her.

At this point, however, she felt prayer rise inside her and felt "a sudden surge of electricity down the back of my neck and into my arms and legs . . . a sparkling feeling of bubbly champagne. . . . " Several months prior to this, she'd had an experience during prayer in which "the strangest experience I ever had" occurred. "I didn't see people anymore, or the priest. There was just this white light, a feeling of absolute love like I'd never felt coursing through me. I felt forgiven and at peace."

Rita also had a near death experience at age nine when she nearly drowned and saw that bright light. It is tempting to wonder if having had a near death experience then made it easier for her to have this healing experience later in life.

Her physician, Dr. Donald Meister, stated, "Spontaneous remissions of MS are possible. The only thing that does not fit in this case is that the permanent damage that occurs with MS does not go away [as it did for Rita]. Whether or not this was divinely inspired is not for me to say. I'd love to know how it happened, and be able to use it again."

A BILLION POINTS OF LIGHT

Dr. Elmer Green, director of the mind-body lab of the Menninger Clinic, and a pioneer of biofeedback research, has measured this healing energy. He conducted a series of experiments on healers to, in his words, "see if it is a bunch of malarkey or something that could be proven." Using a highly sensitive electrical measuring device, he found that some healers' bodies emitted startling momentary surges of eighty, one hundred, or even two hundred volts of electricity during the times they stated they were sending out healing energies. "That's not possible," declared Dr. Green. Except, it happened.

Others have documented the existence of this healing energy. Olga Worrall is one of the most extensively studied healers of our time, producing, under experimental conditions, a variety of effects on both living organisms and inanimate systems. Robert Miller, an industrial research scientist in England, found that water "treated" by Worrall, when examined by infrared spectrophotometry, showed changes suggestive of an alteration in hydrogen bonding, an effect almost identical to that of immersing magnets in the water for several hours. This effect wore off after several hours.

Worrall's own explanation for this effect fits precisely within our theory. The body is not a solid mass, she says. Instead, it is a system of little particles or points of energy separated from one another by space and held in place by an electrically balanced field. When these particles are not in their place, disease is manifested in the body. Spiritual healing is a way of bringing these particles back into harmony.

The most telling evidence is found when we go directly to documented case reports of spiritual healing. We find again and again that the best cases of spiritual healing invariably involve right temporal lobe–mediated experiences such as NDEs, out-of-body experiences, and spiritual visions.

Once again, nothing makes this point quite like a story.

Joe Mayerle, thirty-seven years of age, was diagnosed with fatal lung cancer and told that he had less than a year to live.

Nearly ten years later, one of the doctors who had attended him as a resident ran into Joe.

"Weren't you dying when I last saw you?" he asked Joe.

"I sure was."

"Are you still smoking?"

"Yeah. Want one?"

The doctor was shocked.

"What happened?" he asked.

Joe shrugged and told his tale. After his initial diagnosis, all he could do was lie in bed and mutter over and over, "I am going to die."

He did this for several days, becoming more and more distressed. Then, at the height of his anguish, he suddenly had the sensation of leaving his body and watching himself from a third-person perspective.

"There was incredible meaning in the simplest activity," he told the doctor. "There was such indescribable beauty in the most mundane sights that tears would come to my eyes."

And that was it, he said. He left his body and when he came back, it was no longer the same.

Journalist John Cornwell, in *The Hiding Place of God*, his examination of miraculous healings, had this to say about the healings he documented: "At very best, they appear to involve inexplicable remissions of diseases as opposed to the growth of new organs or limbs. Healing, therefore, involves a dramatic cure process of nature, a return to wholeness, rather than a display of magic. [It is] a return to the template from which we were originally fashioned."

A RETURN TO NORMAL

It is when we study these well-documented cases of healing that we learn its true nature. It is a process that rarely produces true miracles, but instead involves a restoration of normal function. This is why miracle cures so often involve disorders of normal function such as cancer or autoimmune diseases and not such things as growing new limbs. This fits with our theory of the healing mechanism, which involves a restoration of the energy template or morphic field that is responsible for the specifics of the material body.

As a medical scientist, I do not have to rely on my faith or be betrayed by my lack of it in studying faith healing. The scientific evidence documents that our right temporal lobe has the power to heal, especially when activated by an interaction with something most people call "God."

The case of Cindy Zeligman further demonstrates the healing power of the right temporal lobe. As a child, she suffered severe sexual abuse at the hands of a relative. She recalls, "He was taking my body for his own pleasure, against my will. The only way I survived him touching me was to 'leave.' I would float up to the corner of the room and watch him, but it wasn't 'me.'" This is what psychiatrists call dissociation, the splitting of the mind and the body. NDEs, spiritual visions, and out-of-body experiences are all dissociative events.

People who have been abused as children learn to dissociate. Their minds gain the ability to leave their bodies as the result of trauma they undergo. Some researchers say this makes it more likely that they will have NDEs as adults, since their right temporal lobes are already sensitized.

This is what happened to Cindy. As an adult, she and her son were in the basement of their home when a propane tank exploded. She received burns over 90 percent of her body and her son died. With eerie calm, she used her charred finger to dial for help.

"I WOULD REFILL MY BODY WITH WHITE LIGHT . . ."

She was flown by helicopter to a hospital in Denver, Colorado, and had a cardiac arrest en route. She floated out of her charred body and saw it below her, in the helicopter. "I felt like I was in this light, being held by two hands, so warm and loved and at peace, something I had not felt since I was a child," she said. Over the next ten days, she had numerous near death and out-of-body experiences as she fought for life.

After seventy-five days, and twenty-seven operations, she learned mind-body techniques to turn off pain centers. "I would always see myself as healing. I would mentally send emeralds, diamonds, rubies, and sapphires shimmering through my blood stream and Ms. Pacman [from the video game] to cleanse my blood. Then I would refill my body with the white light, to rest, to heal," she explained.

All agree that her recovery was miraculous. I am certain this is, in part, due to the miracles of modern medicine and burn units, and, in part, to the miracle of the healing light she was able to contact during her severe illness.

Yet, as miraculous as her survival was, it was her ability to unlock the healing power of the mind and to connect it with a greater healing energy that facilitated the miracle.

New Orleans burn specialist Dabney Ewin uses the same techniques to heal burn victims. He induces a trance in the patient and helps them control their pain by directing them through guided imagery. Ewin teaches patients to dissociate, to unhook their mind from their body, which seems to be an essential element in the healing process, and to "go to a cave by the ocean, where they feel relaxed, pleasant, free of responsibility" or to go to a "laughing place."

Numerous controlled clinical studies have shown that hypnosis can be useful in controlling injuries from burns. Hypnosis is felt by some to be a state of dissociation, says Stanford University psychiatrist David Spiegel. As such, it is similar to an NDE and perhaps mediated by the same biological structures.

Under hypnosis, patients have been able to speed the healing of burns and wounds. Conversely, thirteen Japanese students, while under hypnosis, were told a plant was highly poisonous. When they touched it, they broke out in blisters and swellings even though the plant was harmless.

In one dramatic case, Dr. Theodore Barber used hypnosis to treat a patient plagued with "fish skin." Fish skin is a usually untreatable condition in which the body is covered with thick scales. Within five days of hypnotherapy, the patient had shed his thick, scaly skin and grown normal skin on 90 percent of his body. Dr. Barber wrote, "At least in some individuals, abnormally functioning skin cells begin to function normally when the individual is exposed to specific words or communications."

HYPNOSIS NOT REQUIRED

It is important for all of us to understand Dr. Barber's final conclusion about hypnosis. He states that it is not a special state of mind but rather a heightened state induced by specific beliefs. Dr. Barber's research has shown that the effects of hypnosis can be obtained simply by asking people to concentrate on a desired goal.

This has enormous implications in that it suggests that our everyday waking thoughts have an enormous impact on our health, for both the good and the bad.

For example, certain personality styles are associated with certain diseases. Dominant, angry, hostile males are more prone to heart attacks, whereas passive, nurturing females who are reluctant to express their angry emotions are more prone to cancer. So, as we study the miraculous, keep in mind that we don't expect these miracles to happen all the time. Rather, they dramatically illustrate the ordinary abilities to heal or harm our bodies that we all have.

THE "BOILING ENERGY" OF HEALTH

Other research on spontaneous healing has confirmed the healing power of this heightened state of mind. Writer and skeptic Ruth Cranston analyzed sixty-five miraculous cures at Lourdes and wrote, "Many spoke of a sense of unawareness, of being transported outside themselves, absorbed in oblivion, all the subjective signs of dissociative states."

Such descriptions are even cross-cultural. The !Kung Bushmen of the Kalahari speak of a healing force they call "boiling energy," which comes from outside the body to heal it.

The *Journal of Medicine and Philosophy* reports that a Mr. Jacobson was cured of a hiatal hernia. Both the hernia and his cure were documented by X rays. He states, "The cure consisted of feeling 'a high voltage energy' touching me on the head. I had a feeling I can only describe as bubbling, boiling water rolling to my fingertips and back."

Nobel Prize–winning surgeon Alexis Carrel, from the Rockefeller Institute, concluded, after studying several spontaneous healings, that there is a place where events of utmost medical importance are occurring, which could throw a new light on the mysterious role of the nervous system.

I believe this area is the right temporal lobe. It is there that our own thoughts interact with the universal energy field, or God. Spiritual healings serve only to alert us to the constant role our minds have in regulating our health.

8

Becoming Your Own Healer

ELECTROMAGNETIC CHANGES THAT FUNCTION IN HEALING
are common among people who've had NDEs.
These are some of the strongest pieces of evidence
connecting the universal mind to the body.

Most of the time these electromagnetic changes
heal only the person they happen to, as was the case
with Rita Klaus, the woman with multiple sclerosis
mentioned in the last chapter.

Other times, people who undergo electromagnetic changes through NDEs actually become healers. With some kind of newly given power, they are
able to affect the health of other people. One such
healer is Dr. Joyce Hawkes, a Seattle biochemist and
healer who had her healing powers awakened by an
NDE.

Dr. Hawkes went to Seattle in 1976, took a job
with a prestigious government agency studying cellular biology, and created an electron microscopy
lab. She was a typical rationalistic, reductionistic
doctor until one day, while working in her home, a

leaded glass window fell on her head. She nearly died and had an NDE in which her mother and grandmother greeted her at the end of the tunnel. She met a being of light in a place that glowed with a mystical inner light.

At first, she completely wrote off the experience, thinking it was the result of having been hit on the head and nothing more.

But, as a result of the NDE, she began to meditate, which led her to see visions. In 1984, she had a vision that she described as a call to healing, one so powerful that it "broke my heart."

"I felt the love so deeply, I had to be a healer," she declared. In 1990, she went to Bali as a tourist. While she was there, native healers introduced themselves to her because they recognized her healing abilities and wanted to mentor her.

She returned to the Seattle area and started giving workshops for physicians, nurses, and other scientists like herself who wanted to learn more about their own healing potential.

I have seen and heard the success stories of many of Dr. Hawkes's patients. But the example I want to use here is a personal one, that of a friend, Sue Volanth.

My relationship with Sue had been a close one because she was there for me when I moved to San Francisco for my pediatric internship. Internships are perhaps the most grueling step on the way to becoming a medical doctor. Mine involved thirty-six-hour shifts and many horrifying surprises.

I could not have survived this year without the friendship of Sue Volanth. She did everything for me, from being my first friend in the city to making sure I had something to eat when I came home exhausted after long shifts.

One Sunday morning, I came home after working forty straight hours. I told her that the hardest thing about my schedule was that I could never have fun just dancing and letting loose on a Saturday night. Sue called up a bunch of our friends, pulled down the apartment shades, put on dancing music, and said, "Come on, Mel, let's make Sunday morning into Saturday night." She was a very uplifting and lively friend.

After becoming a physician and moving to Seattle, I lost track of Sue. One day, I learned to my horror that she had been in a wheelchair for about four years. She was injured on her job as a filmmaker when a heavy piece of equipment fell on her leg. The trauma caused a form of nerve damage called reflex neuromuscular dystrophy (RND). Although initially only her leg was injured, the abnormal strain from attempting to walk eventually damaged her knees and back as well.

I immediately called her and learned that she was being treated by top physicians in New Haven, Connecticut, where she now lived. Yet her condition was deteriorating.

I convinced her to fly to Seattle to meet with Dr. Hawkes. I felt strongly that she should attempt spiritual healing, since it is especially effective in dealing with damage to the body's nervous system. RND involves a disruption in the flow of energy through the body, which throws the entire body off balance. Any sort of treatment would have to involve returning the body to its original energy pattern, unblocking the flow of energies, and allowing the body to heal properly.

Sue flew out to see me, as open-minded as always. I took her to see Dr. Hawkes.

The healer had Sue lie down, then quickly moved her hands over her body, about three to five inches from the surface of her skin. She immediately identified a cold spot in the area of Sue's original injury. Ever the skeptical scientist, I had not told Dr. Hawkes the nature of Sue's problem. I wanted to see for myself if she could detect damage to the nervous system, which she did. She then spent an hour using her own body as a conduit, opening healing channels to bring energy into Sue's body. For the first time in four years, Sue began to walk.

She later entered the University of Washington's prestigious rehabilitation clinic and continued walking therapy, spending six weeks as an in-patient before graduating with only a slight limp.

Sue's recovery is typical of what to expect from this sort of healing. Spiritual intervention was pivotal for her. She had not walked for four years before seeing Dr. Hawkes, and walked after seeing her. Then, given the healing boost she needed, she became a patient at the University of Washington's state-of-the-art rehabilitation clinic, which brought her the rest of the way to restored health.

THE BODY ELECTRIC

We know NDEs are a right-temporal-lobe event from a biological point of view and that they often result in healings. We know that remarkable healings are frequently accompanied by the sensation of alternative energies in the body.

Having a right-temporal-lobe experience involving an interaction with a being of light has been shown to alter the subtle electromagnetic fields surrounding our bodies. This experience can occur within the context of nearly dying, or can be a vivid dream involving the perception of a loving being of light, or can be a spiritual vision. All of these events involve the right temporal lobe and create changes in the body's electromagnetic field. One great example is the number of times my NDE patients have to replace watches because their unique electromagnetic fields have stopped them.

Dr. Elmer Green of the Menninger Clinic is a pioneer in the study of this field, creating a new science of measuring subtle energies. Valerie Hunt, Ph.D., of the University of California at Los Angeles, has also been involved through her invention of sophisticated devices to measure these energies directly.

Dr. Hunt has published studies showing that subtle energy

changes occur during fluctuating states of health. She has found that patients who have had NDEs or other dissociative experiences such as spiritual visions have a distinctive second-energy field, one that vibrates at a frequency different from normal. Her measurements can reliably differentiate healthy patients from patients with minor viral illnesses, major illnesses such as cancer, and psychological states such as depression.

The aspects of this second-energy frequency are quite striking. Magnetic strips on ID badges and credit cards are often interfered with, as are the proper workings of computers and electrical equipment. These are the same clinical effects seen with many healers.

For example, one of my neurologist friends has a patient who is a Reiki healer. One of the other physicians in the building told him he could always tell when that particular patient came in because his computer malfunctioned. This Reiki healer had had an NDE, which presaged her healing abilities. It is not a great stretch to speculate that the same energy source that creates these electromagnetic and subtle energy changes in the human body is also responsible for the subtle energies that lead to spontaneous healings.

SIX LAWS OF HEALING

I have learned from Paul Pearsall the scientific laws he has discovered in his work on "miracle makers." Pearsall is a Ph.D. immunologist who recovered from bone and blood cancer with both the aid of heroic medical intervention and three NDEs. He spent many months in cancer wards and met others like him, whom he called "miracle makers." He feels that six scientific laws govern these miracle makers and are laws all of us need to understand to stay healthy, even if we are not confronted by a life-threatening disease.

Oneness. Miracle makers have a motto, "All are one, in one are all." Essentially, that means we share a piece of the universal energy pattern, or consciousness. Theoretical physicist Erwin Schrödinger, who won the Nobel Prize in 1933, felt it was scientifically correct to conclude that our individual brains contribute to the universal mind. That was what he meant when he coined the term "one mind" to explain the implications of theoretical physics for consciousness research. Pearsall states that a key step to making miracles is to understand the link connecting us all.

Perception. There are many realms of senses and we simultaneously exist in them all. Helen Keller was a miracle maker because, when freed from seeing only with her eyes and hearing with her ears, she could travel and see through many realms of senses. The same is true of having an NDE. The shutdown of input from the five senses allows the brain to perceive other realities. Miracles occur when we bring energy and insights into our lives from those other sensory realms.

Simultaneity. Everything that ever has happened, is happening, and ever will happen is happening all at once. Theoretical physicists have repeatedly tried to explain to us that time is not a fundamental principle of the universe but that simultaneity is. Understanding this explains how the mind can be free from the constraints of distance and time.

Forceful fields. Our lives are shaped and directed by morphic energy fields that we cannot see but that are important in our lives. We can alter these fields with our thoughts, often leading to a restoration of health, or the creation of illness.

Divine dynamics. Energy cannot be created or destroyed. Modern mathematical analysis shows that, as energy flows through systems, disorder ultimately results in a reordering of the system. In other words, stability leads to chaos, which then leads to new stability and then chaos again.

The only constant is the flow of energy through the system. Miracle makers see the disarray of a person's energy as an opportunity to reorganize into a greater stability. This may be the mechanism of the spontaneous resolution of cancers, since cancer is an extreme disorder of cellular function.

Miracle makers love chaos. Chaos is, ultimately, healthy, in that it leads to a new order. This is an extension of the previous point. If chaos is life, you are dead when you reach biological equilibrium. Miracle makers celebrate the paradoxes and the majestic beauty of the whirls, twirls, and scattered flurries of our chaotic lives.

ALL IS ONE

So, what can each one of us learn from the "miracle makers love chaos" findings?

First and foremost, our minds and bodies are interconnected, primarily through emotions and thoughts. Candace Pert, former chief of brain chemistry at the National Institute of Mental Health, discovered dozens of brain hormones and proteins that are secreted in response to our emotions and thoughts, and that have specific actions at hundreds of sites throughout the body. Every time we laugh, cry, or become angry, we are bombarding our body with various neurochemicals that correspond to these emotions.

Yet we know from studies of personality and disease that there are no "good" personality types or thoughts. Each personality extreme has its own particular diseases associated with it. Angry, hostile people who have to be the center of attention have heart attacks. Loving, nurturing people who never express anger or hateful emotions get cancer. Depressed people get pancreatic cancer, while highly emotional people get autoimmune disorders.

Research has shown that it is better to have a balance of

happy, sad, angry, and empathic emotions. People who have lots of friends and close family ties live longer than those who are loners, probably because those family interconnections keep them in balance, exposing them to the entire range of emotions.

So how do we tap in to these emotions to help ourselves? How do we make sure that we don't have an excess of one emotion or another that may cause a disharmony with the original morphic field our bodies are templated from? In short, how do we make sure that our body's energy is balanced in such a way that we are not out of synch with ourselves?

In working with children who have had NDEs, I have devised a series of "rules to live by." These are changes that have consciously or unconsciously taken place in the lives of people who have had NDEs. I have included these ten rules below, providing medical research or concrete advice where possible on how to implement them.

MORPHIC GROUND RULES

By following these rules, it is possible to keep from falling out of synch with our morphic field. When the body is brought back into synch with the original morphic field, disease often melts away, causing remarkable recoveries and spiritual healings. If that is true, then these ten rules for good health could also be called morphic ground rules:

Rule 1: Have lots of friends and connect to a social network. If you don't have a strong social network, volunteer at your local hospital, or join a church or a walking club. It's a more effective and less costly way to feel good than gobbling vitamins and medications.

Dr. Dean Ornish, a San Francisco internist who studies the effects of lifestyle on heart disease, feels that the involvement his patients have in community activities may be the key ingredient to their heart health, possibly being more important than low-fat diets and exercise. Socializing is the most efficient way to expose yourself to the entire range of healthy emotions while remaining in synch with your morphic "stock."

Rule 2: Turn off the verbal mind for a while. Dissociation enhances resonance and communication with the universal mind and one's own morphic field. Virtually any mindless activity involving cessation of the internal narrator will do— needlepoint, tying fishing flies, collecting and organizing stamps, meditation. Singing and ritualistic chanting also serve a similar function.

Turn off the verbal mind for twenty to thirty minutes a day. It is not necessary to do it in an absolutely quiet room. If the internal narrator intrudes, as is inevitable, simply redirect your mind to the activity or say the word "one" (or whatever word you like) over and over until the voice goes away. It is a lot easier to do than you might think.

Rule 3: Use patterns and habits to influence your health. Disruptions in our routine can be hazardous to our health. Any disruptions of the routine, be they positive or negative, have negative effects on health. For example, a promotion, Christmas, a new baby, or a sudden increase in wealth can be as hard on your health as disease, death in the family, or job loss.

Avoiding life stresses isn't the message, but mitigating their impact is. Get into regular, healthy life patterns such as sitting down to eat meals in a relaxed atmosphere three times a day, having regular, repetitive exercise, etc. Make these part of a consistent routine. This is especially true if you are in a period of transition. A regular routine will help keep you healthy.

Rule 4: Have absolute faith in a belief system and stick to it. Remember the Princeton mind-matter studies with the Styrofoam balls? They showed that people who regularly try to influence their environment can do so in subtle ways.

Faith in a belief system is the underlying theme in mind-body interactions. Sir William Osler, the father of modern medicine, said it best: "Faith in gods or saints cures one, faith in little pills another, hypnotic suggestion a third, faith in a plain common doctor a fourth. The faith with which we work has limitations, but it is the most precious commodity."

Rule 5: Stress in our lives is not a health risk factor. It is the feeling of helplessness and lack of power over our own lives that is deadly. The sense that one's life is not important or meaningful is a significant health risk factor.

In one landmark study, mice were injected with a substance known to cause tumors. Some were given random electrical shocks and then allowed to escape the electrodes. Others were given the same number of electrical shocks, but were not given the opportunity to flee after the shock. The second group developed twice as many tumors as the first.

The authors concluded that a sense of learned helplessness is a risk factor in tumor formation. Many other similar animal studies have documented a sense of being in control and making decisions as essential for good health.

Studies of people with high-stress jobs that involve late hours and erratic schedules demonstrate this point. A boss and a secretary can often work the same number of hours and respond to the same deadlines. Yet it is the secretary who typically becomes ill from the job as a result of what researchers call a lack of "decision latitude." So, don't be passive in your life day after day. It is important to your health to make decisions and take control. Even if the decisions are sometimes wrong, they are at least your decisions.

Rule 6: Anger kills and love heals. Having an angry, hostile personality is as important a health risk factor as having high cholesterol. Dr. Redford Williams, a physician at Duke University, showed that 20 percent of physicians with high hostility scores at age twenty-five had died by age fifty, whereas only 2 percent of low scorers had died by that age.

This and other studies like it show that anger and hostility result in diseases of all types. Scientific evidence points to a universe that is a loving one, designed to nurture consciousness. The clinical evidence from those who have had NDEs is that they encounter a blast of pure, unconditional love when their consciousness merges with that light waiting at the point of death.

We know from well-documented studies that spiritual visions such as NDEs heal. We have learned that prayer can heal heart attack patients. Now we can understand exactly why it heals by using the lessons given to us by children who have had NDEs.

As several of the teenagers I have worked with who have had NDEs put it, "All of life is connected. Everything and everyone is important. My life is important because every life is important. Life is for living, and that light is everywhere."

Rule 7: We need to have regular hugs and touches. I know it seems amusing to see buttons that say "A hug a day keeps the doctor away." But studies have documented that people who are hugged or hug three times a day have significantly lower disease rates of all sorts than those who have no hugs. Studies show that premature infants who are massaged grow faster, are healthier, and have better lung function than those who aren't. Oxygen saturation studies show immediate improvement in blood oxygen levels after massage.

Therapeutic touch is a proven remedy that involves touching the energy boundary of the body. For most people, these boundaries extend three to six inches from the physical body. Like meditation, therapeutic touch can be learned quickly and is very effective. Benefit can be seen after a few minutes, especially in people with conditions such as asthma, chronic pain, headaches, and chronic immune disorders. I have prevented more that one asthmatic from being admitted to the intensive care unit by adding therapeutic touch to the treatment regimen.

Rule 8: Don't learn to be ill; teach yourself and your children to be well. Researchers are discovering that many people have "learned" illnesses, or the illness habit. Researchers at Johns Hopkins University have analyzed the way parents respond to a child who is ill with a cold. They found that certain parents give their children presents, toys or treats, when they are sick. The parents often inadvertently give their children the message that illness is a way to get treats and avoid unpleasant tasks. For example, if a child is ill, he does not have to make up homework or tests that were missed because of illness.

When these children are older, they are more likely to have irritable bowel syndrome than the general population. They also are more likely to have painful cramps with menstrual periods (in the case of women) and more viral illnesses.

Another study was done on asthmatic children at the Nation's Children's Hospital in Washington, D.C. The study focused on children who had a genetic tendency to have asthma. Their mothers were interviewed to learn about any stress at home, the stability of their marriages, and their ability to cope with the stresses of working and/or having a baby. There was a 400 percent increase in asthma in the children of stressed parents.

The best strategy is to focus on wellness. The highly successful chronic pain clinic at the University of Washington got patients to see what areas of their lives were actually nourished by their chronic pain. Understanding how patients actually benefit from illness gives them a starting point for learning to be healthy.

We should learn these lessons for our everyday lives, taking a few minutes to analyze how we benefit from whatever ailments and illnesses we have. One reason I overeat is because it is time I can spend alone and totally pamper myself. By learning to pamper myself with a hot bath or a run instead, I lost much of my craving to overeat. Mind-body therapists find a correlation between toxic lifestyle patterns, such as overeating, and emotional needs that those toxic patterns nourish.

We are accustomed to thinking of overeating, for example, as unhealthy. We should take a tip from the pain clinic doctors and analyze why such patterns are healthy for us and what we gain from them, and attempt to substitute other, less toxic behaviors that can achieve the same goal.

Some examples of negative behaviors that can be replaced with positive ones include:

- Working overtime and too late at the office to compensate for a lonely home life. Perhaps joining a chess club or church group would be healthier.

- Drinking to excess to medicate ourselves because we are depressed. It would be healthier to understand the nature of clinical depression and recognize that we have excellent drugs for anxiety and depression that do not create the problems associated with alcohol use.

- Overeating to change our body image. It would be healthy to ask, "How do I benefit by being overweight?" Although this may seem an absurd question, it may result in some amazingly poignant answers that could change your life.

Some people, for example, discover that being overweight is a means of getting attention from a parent who hopes to get them to lose weight. By staying heavy, that person receives the full attention of a concerned parent. Or, many overweight people lose weight and discover that they now have to confront their own sexuality, something they were able to avoid by unconsciously gaining weight.

Many times there are unconscious reasons for obesity. Just as we are what we eat, we also eat as we are. Asking why we eat too much and listening to the first answer that comes to mind can result in life-changing insight.

Rule 9: Learn to meditate or pray regularly. Formal meditative techniques are specifically designed to induce a dissociative, or altered state of consciousness, creating a direct link between our minds and universal energy. It also puts us in touch with the morphic energy field that is the source of our body's biological structure.

One such technique is called "mindful meditation." Rather than turning off the body's internal narrator as we discussed in rule 2, mindful meditation focuses on thoughts, sensations, and physical discomfort. This is a practice developed in Asia more than two thousand years ago as a means to help people cultivate a greater awareness and the wisdom to live each moment to its fullest.

Such a technique is studied at the Stress Reduction Clinic at the University of Massachusetts Medical Center, where people are taught to focus on what is right with them forty-five minutes a day.

The purpose of mindful meditation is not to stop the mind, but to observe it in action. As one of my friends from medical school used to say, "You can't stop the waves, but you can learn to surf."

Mindful eating is a useful technique in losing weight. Overweight individuals often do not taste their food and eat too quickly. Here are examples of how to avoid that:

- *Look at the food*. Acknowledge what it is, how it looks, and where it came from. *Tune in to your breathing as you eat*. Feel the food in your mouth. *Chew slowly*. Define the taste, texture. Note any impulses you have to rush through this mouthful to get on to the next. *Do not resist the urge to wolf down your food or overeat*. Note the feeling in an objective manner. Continue to chew each bite, recognizing that your body wants to get on to the next bite quickly.

- *Before swallowing, actually think about swallowing*. Feel the food in the back of your throat and as it goes down your esophagus.

- *Think about how you are feeling—anxious, depressed, whatever*. Again, do not suppress any thoughts or judge them. Instead, observe as an outsider would. This type of analysis can be extended to any routine daily activity we do without really thinking about it.

Psychologists Joel Weinberger and David McClelland of Boston University document that one profound effect of this training is to foster a sense of connectedness with others and with the universe. As we know, this is also one of the important lessons of NDEs. But this can be achieved not only by nearly dying, but by simply stimulating the right temporal lobe through mindful meditation.

Rule 10: Practice optimism. How can we "learn" to be optimistic, and why is it so important? Again, we can look to NDEs to understand the importance of optimism. Those who have had NDEs have the firm conviction that their lives are important and meaningful. They tend to place unhappy and unpleasant events within a global context or pattern, understanding that bad things can happen to good people and that they are all part of what we call living.

These same attitudes, when observed in people who have not had NDEs, are found to have the same healthful effects as in those who have had NDEs. The Harvard Study of Adult Development is a thirty-five-year study of human personality that began in 1937. It was designed to study personality and emotional health, following the subjects throughout their lives.

The subjects, as college students, underwent a battery of psychological tests and were interviewed by psychiatrists. Significantly, the study found that those subjects who had an optimistic outlook were healthier than their pessimistic counterparts. This was especially seen at age forty-five, but continued throughout life.

A similar study was done at Virginia Polytechnic Institute and found the same results. A third study, at the University of Pennsylvania, went even further and found a significant link between optimism and specific blood studies of the immune system, including helper T-cells and suppressor T-cells. It found that optimistic people fight off infection better than pessimistic ones.

Many other studies document the same effect. Coronary bypass patients who are optimistic about their survival return to work sooner, have a better sex life, and live longer than those who aren't optimistic. Patients paralyzed with spinal cord injuries who have optimistic personalities have a better return of neurological function than those who don't.

A sense of control is also important for good health. Harvard and Yale researchers did a simple study of nursing home patients. They gave half the residents the right to make decisions about their daily lives, such as when to see a movie, what movies to watch, the composition of their meals, and other things. After eighteen months, patients who had more control were happier, more optimistic, and had a 15 percent mortality rate as opposed to a 30 percent mortality rate in the control group who had to follow the nursing home regime.

This is a landmark study showing that we can alter our personality through simple actions and that these simple actions can profoundly affect our health. In the Harvard-Yale nursing home study, patients were randomly assigned to either group. The optimistic group learned to be optimistic from being given more control over their lives.

Pessimistic people often are those who have not learned the lessons of children who have had NDEs. When something bad happens, they are unable to put it in a global context. They immediately generalize, saying, "See, everything bad happens to me."

As a general rule, optimists use specific external explanations for negative or unpleasant events. Pessimists tend toward internal and global explanations. For example, a man approaches a woman at a party and asks her out. She rejects him dismissively. The pessimist's response is something like "Sometimes I am boring," or "I am unattractive."

In contrast, the optimist thinks, "She was in a rejecting

mood." This implies that she might be interested the next time, or that someone else might be. The pessimist blames himself for the rejection. The optimist sees the experience within a greater context, thinking the problem might be with the other person.

Other studies show that children can be taught to be optimistic. This can be achieved by helping them to see failure as a chance to do better, challenging their pessimistic views, screening their friends and teachers for pessimistic tendencies, and teaching them not to generalize from failure.

BRINGING IT TOGETHER

Understanding the underpinnings of NDEs is a key to improving our everyday health and to bringing the healing power of optimism, trust, and love into our daily lives.

The National Institute of Discovery Science, of which I am a member, is currently outlining an experimental agenda for consciousness research. One area we are studying is the effects of NDEs on the human immune system.

One of the people we are studying is Paul Carr, who was an auditor for the state of California when he nearly died from a heart attack. Before his NDE, he was very overweight, felt angry all the time, and worked in a dark office because his depression wouldn't allow him to tolerate light. After his NDE, he told me he could no longer return to the dark room that was his workplace. The unhappiness that it represented was simply too great.

He developed a love of talking to people as a result of his NDE and went on to become a highly successful real estate broker. He enjoyed the challenge of matching potential home buyers with their perfect home. He went from being very linear and counting columns of numbers all day to being more of a global thinker and seeing the interconnections of life.

Carr feels that his NDE made him healthier, and in meeting him and examining his medical records it is impossible to argue with him. For Carr, renewed health has come from the lessons he learned from nearly dying: Live life to its fullest; pay attention to what is going on around you; and believe that, in the long run, everything has a purpose and works out for the best.

These are all aspects of a healthy personality, which can be achieved without an NDE. You just need to know that they are important and that you can adapt them to your life if you really try.

There is an old saying, "What you see is what you become." I believe it means that our attitude about life shapes our lives. It makes sense and is clearly connected to love. If a child grows up unloved, he is an unhappy, angry adult who will be likely to have health problems.

Activating the right temporal lobe helps to make us better people because we become totally aware of the world around us and the meaning behind the things we previously ignored. In doing so, we discover that we all have an inner source of healing—a secret helper—that is always present and operating on an unconscious level.

The ultimate message of NDEs is that life has meaning and that we are all connected. It is in finding these interconnections that we find the secret to good health and a long life.

9

Trusting Your Feelings

> The whole "spirit world," death, all these things
> that are so closely related to us, have through
> our daily defensiveness been so entirely pushed
> out of life that the sense with which we might
> have been able to grasp them has atrophied.
>
> —*Rainer Maria Rilke*

IN MY NEAR DEATH STUDIES, I REPEATEDLY HEAR A SIMILAR recurrent theme: *Listen to that voice in your head.*

One such voice came to a physician who was getting on a plane to go to a conference in New Orleans. While saying good-bye to his infant son, he distinctly heard a voice saying, "You will never see him again." It was not an ordinary thought, or the unconscious rendering of a fear. He'd had many of the latter sorts of thoughts in which he would dwell on an irrational fear or think about his child dying. This was totally different. It was a loud voice in his head, so loud he looked around, thinking others could hear it.

Sadly, the voice he heard was correct. His infant son died of sudden infant death syndrome while he was at that conference.

Another story came to me from a doctor I work with. One night, he left the hospital for his drive home and stopped at a red light at a deserted intersection. When the light turned green, he suddenly felt a fear so deep in his stomach that he thought he would throw up. His heart was beating rapidly, he began to sweat profusely, and he could not take his foot off the brake.

Suddenly, a car came hurtling through the red light and across the intersection. Had he accelerated when the light turned green he would have been hit and probably killed by the speeding car. He called this a case of "sensory intuition." As he put it: "I didn't hear a voice that told me not to move, but my other senses did."

Defined as "arriving at decisions or conclusions without conscious or explicit processes of reasoned thinking," intuition is perhaps the least controversial of our paranormal abilities. Even a game like bridge has intuition or hunches built into it. In an effort to be fair, players who use hunches on a regular basis are required to disclose this to other players. This bridge rule is proof of the existence of intuition, since there would not be such a rule unless players regularly made decisions based on hunches.

To date, no well-described attempt to identify the source of hunches or intuitions has been found. The best attempts to explain intuition have assumed that it represents the unconscious mind gathering and interpreting sensory input that is not always consciously interpreted. As we will see, intuition, in fact, represents the input from a completely different source than the five known senses. It represents our ability to interact directly with a nonlocal reality, also known as God.

NORMAL ACTIVITY

Intuition is the normal function of the right temporal lobe. The essence of intuition is that there is a direct connection between the human mind and a universal mind, a direct connection between the organized patterns of energy that represent ourselves and the entire pattern in which we are embedded.

By learning about intuition we learn to reconnect with God and rediscover meaning in our lives. This is the most essential function of the right temporal lobe. It is not to make accurate stock market predictions, or move tiny pieces of metal; rather, it is to bring meaning and purpose to our lives, to do nothing less than reconnect us with what most people call God.

ON THE BEAT

So what does the right temporal lobe do? The best-documented function of the right temporal lobe is its role in processing and interpreting memory. Intuition relies heavily on the right temporal lobe's ability to recall virtually every detail of the brain's perceptions, even though most memories are never consciously processed. For example, a policeman walks into a convenience store and intuitively feels that a robbery is going to take place. Many policemen describe such feelings and as a result have the ability to act quickly. Indeed, it is this sort of commonplace event that firmly establishes the existence of intuition. But what exactly is happening within a police officer's mind to create such life-saving intuitions?

In the convenience-store robbery example, what the policeman perceives as intuition is often a combination of training; subliminal perceptions of clues, such as a car with the engine running and an impatient driver; and the anxious look on the clerk's face. This ability to comprehend and assess an event is essential to intuition.

When we use our right temporal lobe, we directly perceive a reality unfiltered by input from the five senses. The input from those perceptions fuels intuition. Not surprisingly, most of our actions and decisions are based not on our logical left temporal lobe, but on our sixth sense. This is why we have learned to trust our intuitions or listen to inner voices. These voices represent information coming to us from the nonlocal, right–temporal–lobe–mediated reality. Intuition is not just the subliminal processing of memory, but also incorporates all of the right-temporal-lobe abilities.

Remote viewing, telepathy, precognition, déjà vu, telekinesis, and after-death communications all function to increase our sense of empathy and our perception of our environment. The gift of communicating with angels, and God, has an obvious benefit in intuitive decision making.

We have all used our intuition. Yet, until now, there has been no comprehensive attempt to explain how intuition works and what areas of the brain mediate it. Prior to this book, it has been assumed to be nonrational and, ultimately, unexplainable, similar to the way in which spiritual or religious people speak of their experiences.

Here is what Richard Gregory, professor of neuropsychology and director of the Brain and Perception Laboratory in Bristol, England, has to say about intuition: "It is sometimes thought intuitions are reliable, and indeed, we do act most of the time without knowing why or what our reasons may be. It is certainly rare to set out an argument in formal terms, and go through the steps set forth by logicians. In this sense, almost all judgments and behaviors are intuitive. The term is used in philosophy to denote the alleged power of the mind to see certain self-evident truths. The status of intuition has declined over the last century, perhaps with the increasing emphasis on formal logic, explicit data and assumptions of science."

It is precisely for this reason that all of the specific components of intuition are, in themselves, poorly understood and often dismissed or ignored. We have forgotten about intuition. It is no longer an important part of modern life, or so we think.

SENSITIVE LOBE

Yet intuition is the cornerstone of personal safety. Gavin de Becker, the security expert mentioned earlier, feels that intuition is your most important line of defense against personal assault. De Becker says, "Intuition connects us to the natural world and to our nature. Freed from the bonds of judgment, married only to perception, it carries us to predictions we will later marvel at."

It may be hard to accept the importance of intuition because it is usually looked upon by thoughtful Westerners as emotional, unreasonable, or inexplicable. Husbands often chide their wives about feminine intuition and do not take it seriously. We much prefer logic, the grounded, explainable, unemotional thought process that ends in a supportable conclusion. In fact, Americans worship logic, even when it's wrong, and deny intuition, even when it's right.

This is a recurrent theme throughout our analysis of right-temporal-lobe talents. Since so many of us do not believe there is any consciousness, or God, outside our own minds, the input from the sensing organ for the perception of that same God seems suspect. We feel foolish believing in it and think we are being irrational.

Yet people who've had NDEs know the power of intuition. Indeed, a powerful spiritual experience like an NDE activates the atrophied neurons in our right temporal lobes. After such an experience, the entire lobe is sensitized. Suddenly, instead of just inputting sensory data from the immediate local world, all of the information from nonlocal reality pours in. As Dr. Raymood Moody, psychiatrist and death researcher, once said, "It is as if your television set can tune in one hundred channels and does so all at once."

CHANNEL SURFING

Right-temporal-lobe sensitivity and the resulting telepathy, telekinesis, remote viewing, and precognition provide powerful, useful information about our immediate world. No wonder many people who have had NDEs go on to become inventors, rock stars, film producers, and other successful and creative beings.

"Intuition is the power of obtaining knowledge that cannot be acquired either by inference or observation, by reason or experience," says the *Encyclopaedia Britannica*. "As such, intuition is thought of as an original, independent source of knowledge."

To my way of thinking, intuition represents the sensory input of nonlocal reality blended with other right-temporal-lobe functions. The right temporal lobe is the only sensory organ for paranormal reality that we have.

Again, from the *Encyclopaedia Britannica*, "Intuition is designed to account for just those kinds of knowledge that other sources do not provide."

Some modern anthropologists feel that primitive man exhibited paranormal talents, including precognition, out-of-body states, remote viewing, shamanistic voyages, spiritual visions, and telepathy, as well as access to all types of knowledge well beyond their abilities in direct observation. Certainly, this was a survival advantage. And one characteristic we all share is our highly evolved right temporal lobe, which distinguishes us from lower primates.

For most of human history, right-temporal-lobe functions dominated and left-temporal-lobe functions, such as language and writing, were almost nonexistent. We know that both temporal lobes evolved at the same time, perhaps two hundred thousand years ago. For preindustrial man, right-temporal-lobe abilities were more important for survival than they are today. Remote viewing helped in giving general perceptions of where herds of animals might be. In certain primitive tribes even today, remote viewing is used to hunt for animals.

Think of some of humanity's astonishing migrations, such as the first humans who came across from Siberia to Alaska on the land bridge. They walked for thousands of miles through a narrow chasm in glacial ice, where food was sparse. Indeed, the entire concept of such a migration was thought by the scientific establishment to be laughable until DNA studies on Native Americans proved that the Americas were populated by successive waves of small bands of people from Asia. Woudn't such a migration seem more possible if they were telepathically linked, had remote viewing, telekinesis, and precognition?

LOBE SHIFTING

When did it happen that humans shifted from being primarily right-temporal-lobe to left-temporal-lobe oriented? One of the best historical analyses of this question was done by Princeton psychologist Julian Jayne, Ph.D., who has studied the physiology of consciousness.

Dr. Jayne theorized that early humans did not have an individual sense of consciousness. They were so linked to each other and to the universe that they thought of themselves as sharing consciousness, not only with other humans but with everything in the universe. Dr. Jayne defines consciousness as the "I" each one of us has and takes for granted.

The Vikings adhered to the early human concept of a shared community and "group thinking." Yet each individual had a particular skill that he or she used to contribute to society as a whole. Often, individuals were known by their profession—the blacksmith, the baker, the king, the serf, the warrior.

Yet each individual was firmly embedded in a structured society and understood his or her relationship to that structure.

Individual consciousness occurred because of a dysfunction within the human brain. Modern man, in spite of all of our accomplishments, is brain imbalanced. Dr. Jayne has shown that the origins of human consciousness came from a breakdown in the proper integration of the right and left temporal lobes, which explains why he titled his book *The Origins of Consciousness in the Breakdown of the Bicameral Mind*. The bicameral mind is the mind humans had for the first 195,000 years of their existence. It has been in the past 5,000 years that we have suffered from a lack of communication between the two sides of the brain, leaving an unhealthy dominance of the left temporal lobe and a relative atrophy of the right temporal lobe.

When we think of being part of a communal mind, we think of cults or senseless group thinking. That's because we are dominated by the concept of individual consciousness and have neglected, at least in a conscious way, our connections with each other and with the divine. People need a strong sense of individual consciousness. If they don't have it, they do not do well in our society. Children who do not have a strong sense of "I" can, to their detriment, have their needs overlooked and ignored.

That sort of neglect did not often happen in early human societies. Individuals had specific rights and obligations unique to their situations. They did not have to learn to assert themselves. We still see elements of this "old way" of thinking in small towns or isolated areas of our Western culture.

HEALING ENERGY

Three examples of this come from Diane Craig, a registered nurse who has been on the staff of the University of Washington for ten years. Early in her training, she spent considerable time in isolated rural areas, including Appalachia, Peru, and on a Shoshone reservation in Wyoming. She had the opportunity to work closely with a small-town doctor named Dr. Little in Appalachia, a shaman in Peru, and Native American healers in Wyoming.

The one thread common to all three is that they had the unquestioned trust and faith of their patients. In these communities, there was only one healer and everyone knew there was only one way to get well—through the help of that healer.

Craig, who is a thoroughly rational and Western-trained nurse, says, without hesitation, that all three healers used direct energy channeled from the universe to heal patients. She wrinkles her nose, almost in disgust, as she says these words. Craig, like most modern health professionals, believes discussing healing energies is not scientific. Her testimony is all that more valuable because of her intense skepticism.

In Appalachia, she saw an elderly diabetic patient with a severely gangrenous foot. She said Dr. Little told her that they had to work quickly and all night to save it. She felt it was a waste of time. She had seen such gangrene before and had only seen it managed by amputation. Dr. Little told her to go into the backyard and gather an herb that he called a "marshmallow plant." With the herb, they made a poultice that was applied directly to the leg. By morning, normal color had returned to the foot and the gangrene was gone. She described Dr. Little as a man "whose word was the gospel." Whatever he said, people believed. He was humble, unassuming, and very much a humanitarian. She believed that energy directly flowed from his body into patients and claims to have personally perceived this happening on more than one occasion.

As a nursing missionary in Peru, Craig was assigned to teach nutrition and prenatal care. After a few months, she realized that the local population did not respect her and was unwilling to work with her. She introduced herself to the elders in the community, especially the local shaman, and worked closely with him. After she gained his confidence and respect, she had an easier time teaching nutrition and prenatal care. The shaman was flamboyant, and was more interested in making money and having power and respect. He used religious rituals and, at times, was known to put a hex on someone, which immediately resulted in poor health. Even though his personality and methods were different from Dr. Little's, the outcomes were much the same.

At one point she saw a child with an obvious ear infection, one with pus draining from the site of the infection. The shaman rolled some herbs and what seemed to be gunpowder into a ball. Then he took a piece of paper, rolled it into a funnel, and placed the tip in the child's ear. He put the mixture in the funnel and set it on fire. When the fire reached the gunpowder, it gave out a loud bang. He pulled the funnel away from the ear and pronounced the child cured. Craig personally witnessed that the drainage from the ear, and the infection, disappeared over the next few hours.

The native healers in the Shoshone community were different still. They relied heavily on inducing out-of-body experiences, using right-temporal-lobe stimulants such as peyote. While in these trances they were able to focus and channel healing energies. She saw stroke patients successfully treated in this fashion.

Craig's experiences precisely illustrate the true nature of right-temporal-lobe function and spiritual healing. What is important is the concept of a healer as a revered, respected member of the society, and that everyone in the society has a shared concept of what that healer's role is.

SPECIFIC ENERGIES

The specifics of how that healer performs cures are unique to his or her personality and the culture. Dr. Little used herbs and poultices; the shaman, magic tricks; and the Native American healers, peyote and trances. All healers got the same results. The common factor was that each believed there was a transfer of energy between the healer and the patient. This type of healing can work only when everyone is connected with the same model of the universe.

The common thread in these remedies is that each was used in a communal context in which there was complete faith that the remedy would work. If Dr. Little tried to use peyote to induce a healing trance or did magic tricks with gunpowder, he could not have achieved the same cure rate. If a university-trained physician treated gangrene with herbs, he would probably fail. Seeing what does work gives us insights into this link between individual consciousness and the collective consciousness. We all share a culturally received perception of what defines healing and how it works. This shared perception is telepathically communicated through our right temporal lobes.

On this final point, Craig is very clear. She states that it was not that the patients believed the remedies would work, but it was her perception that there was some sort of interaction with patients on an energy, or spiritual, level. She felt Dr. Little had a natural ability and needed no rituals or embellishments, and that both the shaman and the Native American healers used techniques not to induce a state of belief, but to induce a state of consciousness within themselves that allowed their healing energies to flow.

THE EVER-EVOLVING BRAIN

The challenge now is to do what mystics, healers, and, yes, even children who have had NDEs have done, which is to learn how to integrate both the rational and the spiritual sides of our brains. As it now stands, we lean very heavily on pragmatic information to make our decisions. If a decision isn't "science based," it is often thought to be an inferior one. We not only ignore the intuitive and spiritual voices in our heads, we criticize them as if they were delivering the impressions of fools.

In short, we act like a two-headed person arguing with himself, which, in essence, is what we are. We have, after all, two completely separate hemispheres to our brains that are connected by thick bundles of neurons.

The brain's two sides do not operate independently. The two temporal lobes have their own way of communicating with each other via large bundles of nerve cells called the anterior commissure. As Dr. Jayne states, "In man, there is a band of fibers from the left temporal lobe . . . which connects with the other temporal lobe. Here, then, I suggest, is the tiny bridge across which came the directions which built our civilizations and founded the world's religions, where gods spoke to men and were obeyed. . . ."

ALL THE EQUIPMENT NECESSARY

The neuroanatomy necessary to perceive the divine is all there. Our reliance on the "rational world" comes from the fact that modern man is truly not using the right temporal lobe.

About five thousand years ago, religion was born because most people no longer heard the voice of God and only certain individuals were recognized as having that ability. This evolved to the present day, where only people who lived in earlier times are recognized as having heard the true word of

God. People who claim to hear God's voice these days are considered crazy. By not using our right temporal lobe, we are cut off from one of the most important sources of information we have—nonlocal reality, or, in spiritual terms, God's grace.

More people are beginning to realize this and are becoming intensely interested in events of a mystical nature like near death experiences. NDEs are a gateway to understanding the mystical secrets of the universe. From NDEs we are learning that everyone has the ability to connect with a divine universe. We also are learning that we do not have to wait until we die to connect with this universe. Rather, we can connect with the mystical universe any time during our lives.

Connecting with this universe is my personal challenge. I do not want to wait until I die to learn to hear God's voice.

OWNER'S MANUAL FOR THE BRAIN

I started my research by listening to the NDEs of children and discovered from them that all of us have access to untapped spiritual potential that can transform our lives. By being open to the world around us and the intuitions that come from inside, we can transcend our five senses and reach for an expanded human consciousness, a sort of sixth sense. Once this has occurred, our perspective on life is altered, just as it would be if we suddenly gained eyesight after a lifetime of being blind. This "sudden sight" often precipitates a state of spiritual emergency. Insights and intuitions we have been dismissing or trivializing suddenly take on a larger role in shaping our lives.

When I say intuition I mean nothing less than the ability to communicate directly with God, and to bring spiritual insight and meaning into our lives. This means, of course, the ability to learn to use our entire brain, something we have never done in the entire history of humankind.

Early humans were too dominated by the right temporal lobe. People did not express their own personalities to the extent they do now, and society dominated individuals. Then we became too left-brain dominated. Now we have become too individualistic, and many of our societal problems come from an excessive emphasis on the individual.

NDEs are a wake-up call reminding us that we are interconnected spiritual beings as well as unique individuals. Work on your spiritual sensitivity, but be patient. Although our modern brain began evolving more than two hundred thousand years ago, it didn't come with a manual. We are just starting to learn to use it fully.

THIS BIBLIOGRAPHY REPRESENTS ROUGHLY HALF THE BOOKS and papers I read in preparing this volume. I do not mean this to be an all-inclusive bibliography, but rather a starting place for further research. My newsletter, *Transformations*, is a monthly summary of children's stories, cutting-edge research, and perspectives from areas as diverse as studies of Australian aborigines and UFO research. My newsletter can be subscribed to through my website, Melvinmorse.com, or by writing to Transformations, 3208 Sixth Ave., Tacoma, WA 98406.

This book presents a new scientific theory that I first presented to the medical and scientific community. The scientific paper this book is based on was first presented at an International Conference on Consciousness in Tokyo, and then in the journal *Network* in December 1998. (See "Journals," pp. 188–90.) Copies of the scientific article and references can be found on my website.

SCIENTIFIC AND MEDICAL REFERENCES

Books

Ader, R., D. Felten, and N. Cohen, eds. *Psychoneuroimmunology.* 2d ed. San Diego: Academic Press, 1991.

Andreasen, N. *The Broken Brain: The Biological Revolution in Psychiatry.* New York: Perennial, 1984.

Becker, R. *Cross Currents: The Perils of Electropollution, the Promise of Electromedicine.* Los Angeles: Jeremy P. Tarcher, 1990.

Becker, R., and G. Selden. *The Body Electric: Electromagnetism and the Foundation of Life.* New York: William Morrow, 1985.

Burke, J. *The Day the Universe Changed.* Boston: Little, Brown, 1985.

Calvin, W. *The Ascent of Mind: Ice Age Climates and the Evolution of Intelligence.* New York: Bantam Books, 1990.

Changeux, J.-P. *Neuronal Man: The Biology of Mind.* New York: Oxford University Press, 1985.

Duve, C. de. *Vital Dust: Life as a Cosmic Imperative.* New York: Basic Books, 1995.

Eccles, J. *Evolution of the Brain: Creation of the Self.* New York: Routledge, 1989.

Franklin, J. *Molecules of the Mind: The Brave New Science of Molecular Psychology.* New York: Laurel, 1987.

Gardener, H. *The Mind's New Science: A History of the Cognitive Revolution.* New York: Basic Books, 1985.

Gleick, J. *Chaos: Making a New Science.* New York: Penguin Books, 1987.

Hobson, J. A. *The Dreaming Brain.* New York: Basic Books, 1988.

Hooper, J., and D. Teresi. *The Three-Pound Universe: The Brain, from the Chemistry of the Mind to the New Frontiers of the Soul.* New York: Dell Publishing, 1986.

Jaynes, J. *The Origins of Consciousness in the Breakdown of the Bicameral Mind.* Boston: Houghton Mifflin, 1976.

Jung, C. *Memories, Dreams, Reflections.* New York: Vintage Books, 1963.

Kaku, M. *Hyperspace.* New York: Anchor Books, 1994.

Kosslyn, S. M., and O. Koenig. *Wet Mind: The New Cognitive Neuroscience.* New York: The Free Press, 1992.

Michael, M., W. T. Boyce, and A. Wilcox. *Biomedical Bestiary.* Boston: Little, Brown, 1984.

Moody, R. *Life after Life.* New York: Bantam Books, 1988.

Neppe, V. M. *Cry the Beloved Mind: A Voyage of Hope.* Seattle: Peanut Butter Publishing, 1999.

Penfield, W., and T. Rasmussen. *The Cerebral Cortex of Man: A Clinical Study of Localization of Function.* New York: Macmillan, 1950.

Persinger, M. *Neuropsychological Bases of God Beliefs.* New York: Praeger Publishers, 1987.

Plum, F. P., and J. B. Posner. *The Diagnosis of Stupor and Coma.* 2d ed. Contemporary Neurology Series. Philadelphia: F. A. Davis Co., 1972.

Reiser, M. *Mind, Brain, Body: Toward a Convergence of Psychoanalysis and Neurobiology.* New York: Basic Books, 1984.

Restak, R. *The Brain: The Last Frontier.* New York: Warner Books, 1979.

————.*The Brain.* New York: Bantam Books, 1984.

————.*The Mind.* New York: Bantam Books, 1988.

Sheldrake, R. *A New Science of Life.* Rochester, VT.: Park Street Press, 1987.

Taylor, G. *The Natural History of the Mind.* New York: Penguin, 1979.

Winson, J. *Brain and Psyche: The Biology of the Unconscious.* New York: Vintage Books, 1985.

Articles

Bohm, D., and B. Hiley. "The Causal Interpretation of Quantum Theory." In *Science, Order and Creativity,* by D. Bohm and F. D. Peat. New York: Bantam Books, 1987.

Carr, D. "Pathophysiology of Stress-induced Limbic Lobe Dysfunction: A Hypothesis for NDEs." *Anabiosis: The Journal of Near-death Studies* 2 (1982): 75–90.

Cushing. H.W. *Brain* 44 (1921–22): 341–44.

————. *Transactions of the American Neorologic Association* (1921): 374–75.

Devinsky, O., E. Feldman, and K. Burrowes. "Autoscopic Phenomena with Seizures." *Archives of Neurology* 46 (1989): 1080–88.

Dewhurst, K., and A. W. Beard. "Sudden Religious Conversions in Temporal Lobe Epilepsy." *British Journal of Psychiatry* 117 (1970): 497–507.

Gloor, P., A. Olivier, L. F. Quesney, et al. "The Role of the Limbic System in Experimental Phenomena of Temporal Lobe Epilepsy." *Annals of Neurology* 23 (1982): 129–44.

Halgren, E., R. D. Walter, D. G. Cherlow, et al. "Mental Phenomena Evoked by Electrical Stimulation of the Human Hippocampal Formation and Amygdala." *Brain* 101 (1978): 83–117.

Hameroff, S. R. "Fundamentality: Is the Conscious Mind Subtly Linked to a Basic Level of the Universe?" *Trends in Cognitive Sciences* 2, no. 4 (1998): 119–27.

————. "Quantum Computing in Microtubules: An Intraneural Corre-
late of Consciousness?" *Cognitive Studies* (Bulletin of the Japanese
Cognitive Science Society) 4, no. 3 (1998): 67–92.

Harroldsson, E., and L. R. Gissurarson. "Does Geomagnetic Activity
Affect Extrasensory Perception?" *Personality and Individual Differences* 8 (1987): 745–47.

Hennsley, J. A., P. J. Christenson, R. A. Hardoin, et al. "Premonitions of
Sudden Infant Death Syndrome: A Retrospective Case Control
Study." Abstract in *Pediatr Pulmonol* 16 (1993): 393.

Horrax, G. "Visual Hallucinations as a Cerebral Localizing Phenomenon: With Especial Reference to Their Occurrence in Tumors of the
Temporal Lobes." *Archives of Neurology and Psychiatry* 10, (1923):
532–47.

J. H. Jackson and C. G. Beevor. "Localizing Aspects of Temporal Lobe
Tumors." *Brain* 12 (1889–90): 346–48.

Jansen, K. "Neuroscience, Ketamine, and the Near-death Experience."
In *The Near-death Reader*, edited by L. W. Bailey and J. Yates. New
York: Routledge, 1996.

Kelleher, C. "Retrotranspons as Engines of Human Bodily Transformation." *Journal of Scientific Exploration* (forthcoming).

Kennedy. *Arch Int Med* 8 (1911): 317.

Makarec, K., and M. A. Persinger. "Electroencephalographic Validation
of a Temporal Lobe Signs Inventory in a Normal Population." *Journal
of Research in Personality* 24 (1990): 323–37.

Mendez, M. P., B. Engebrit, and R. Doss. "The Relationship of Epileptic
Auras and Psychological Attributes." *Journal of Neuropsychiatry and
Clinical Neurosciences* 8 (1996): 287–92.

Morgan, H. "Dostoyevsky's Epilepsy: A Case Report and Comparison."
Surg Neurol 33 (1990): 413–16.

Morse, M. L. "Near-death Experiences and Death-related Visions:
Implications for the Clinician." *Current Problems in Pediatrics* (Feb-
ruary 1994): 55–83.

Morse, M. L., P. Castillo, and D. Venecia. "Childhood Near-death Experiences." *American Journal of Diseases of Children* 140 (1986):
110–14.

Morse, M. L., and V. M. Neppe. "Near-death Experiences." Letter in
Lancet 337 (1991): 86.

Morse, M. L., D. Venecia, and J. Milstein. "Near-death Experiences: A
Neurophysiological Explanatory Model." *Journal of Near-death Studies* 8, no. 1 (1989): 45–53.

Mullin, S., and W. Penfield. "Illusions of Comparative Interpretation and Emotion." *Archives of Neurology and Psychology* 81 (1959): 269–85.

Palmini, A., and P. Gloor. "The Localizing Value of Auras in Partial Seizures." *Neurology* 42 (1992): 801–6.

Penfield, W. "Functional Localization in Temporal and Deep Sylvian Areas." In *Research Publications*, vol. 35, edited by H. C. Solomon, S. Cobb, and W. Penfield. New York: New York Association for Research in Nervous and Mental Disease, 1954.

———. "The Role of the Temporal Cortex in Certain Psychical Phenomena." *Journal of Mental Science* 101 (1955): 451–65.

Persinger, M. A., and K. Makarec. "Complex Partial Epileptic Signs as a Continuum from Normal to Epileptics: Normative Data and Clinical Populations." *Journal of Clinical Psychology* 49 (1993): 33–45.

Saver, J. L., and J. Rabin. "The Neural Substrates of Religious Experience." *Journal of Neuropsychiatry* 9 (1997): 498–510.

Schenk, L., and D. Bear. "Multiple Personality and Related Dissociative Phenomena in Patients with Temporal Lobe Epilepsy." *American Journal of Psychiatry* 138 (1981): 1311–16.

Van Buren, J. M. "Sensory, Motor and Autonomic Effects of Mesial Temporal Stimulation in Man." *Journal of Neurosurgery* 18 (1961): 273–88.

Whinnery, J. E. "Methods for Describing and Quantifying +Gz-induced Loss of Consciousness." *Aviation, Space and Environmental Medicine* 60 (1989): 798–802.

———. "Observations on the Neurophysiological Theory of Acceleration-induced Loss of Consciousness." *Aviation, Space and Environmental Medicine* 60 (1989): 589–93.

Whinnery, J. E., and A. M. Whinnery. "Acceleration-induced Loss of Consciousness." *Archives of Neurology* 47 (1990): 764–76.

Williams, D. "The Structure of Emotions Reflecting in Epileptic Experiences." *Brain* 79 (1956): 29–67.

REFERENCES CONCERNING DEATH-RELATED VISIONS, INCLUDING PREMONITIONS, NEAR DEATH EXPERIENCES, AND AFTER-DEATH COMMUNICATIONS

Books

Bailey, L., and J. Yates. *The Near-Death Experience: A Reader.* New York: Routledge, 1996.

Barret, W. *Deathbed Vision: The Psychical Experiences of the Dying.* Wellingborough, Northhamptonshire, England: The Aquarian Press, 1986.

Blackmore, S. *Dying to Live: Near-Death Experiences.* New York: Prometheus Books, 1993.

Cressy, J. *The Near-Death Experience: Mysticism or Madness?* Hanover, Mass.: The Christopher Publishing House, 1994.

Fenwick, P., and E. Fenwick. *The Truth in the Light: An Investigation of Over 300 Near-Death Experiences.* London: Headline Book Publishing, 1995.

Franz, M.-L. von. *On Dreams and Death.* Boston: Shambhala, 1984.

Hoffman, E. *Visions of Innocence: Spiritual and Inspirational Experiences of Childhood.* Boston: Shambhala, 1992.

Horchler, J., and R. Morris. *The SIDS Survival Guide.* Hyattsville, Md.: SIDS Educational Services, 1994.

Iverson, J. *In Search of the Dead: A Scientific Investigation of Evidence for Life After Death.* New York: Harper San Francisco, 1992.

Kircher, P. *Love Is the Link.* Arlington, Va.: Larson Publications, 1995.

Komp, D. M. *A Window to Heaven: When Children See Life in Death.* Grand Rapids, Mich.: Zondervan, 1992.

LaGrand, L. *After-Death Communication: Final Farewells.* St. Paul, MN.: Llewellyn Publications, 1997.

Lee, J. *Death and Beyond in the Eastern Perspective.* An Interface Book. New York: Gordon and Breach, 1974.

Lundahl, C. *A Collection of Near-Death Research Readings.* Chicago: Nelson-Hall Inc., 1982.

Martin, J., and P. Romanowski. *Our Children Forever: George Anderson's Messages from Children on the Other Side.* New York: Berkley Publishing Group, 1994.

———. *We Are Not Forgotten: George Anderson's Messages of Love and Hope from the Other Side.* New York: G. P. Putnam's Sons, 1991.

Moody, R. *Life after Death.* New York: Bantam Books, 1975.

Moody, R., and P. Perry. *Closer to the Light: Learning from the Near-Death Experiences of Children.* New York: Villard Books, 1990.

———. *Parting Visions.* New York: Harper Paperbacks, 1994.

———. *Reunions: Visionary Encounters with Departed Love Ones.* New York: Villard Books, 1993.

———. *Transformed by the Light.* New York: Ivy Books, 1992.

Negovsky, V. A. *Resuscitation and Artificial Hypothermia.* New York: New York Consultants Bureau, 1962.

Osis, K., and E. Harraldsson. *At the Hour of Death.* New York: Avon, 1977.

Rawlings, M. *Before Death Comes*. Nashville: Thomas Nelson, 1980.
———. *Beyond Death's Door*. Nashville: Thomas Nelson, 1978.
———. *To Hell and Back: Life After Death—Startling New Evidence*. Nashville: Thomas Nelson, 1993.
Ring, K. *Heading Toward Omega: In Search of the Meaning of the Near-Death Experience*. New York: William Morrow, 1984.
———. *Life at Death: A Scientific Investigation*. New York: Quill, 1982.
Ring, K., and S. Cooper. *MindSight: Near-Death and Out-of-Body Experiences in the Blind*. Palo Alto, Calif.: William James Center for Consciousness Studies Institute of Transpersonal Psychology, 1999.
Ring, K., and E. Valarino. *Lessons from the Light: What We Can Learn from the Near-Death Experience*. New York: Plenum Press, 1998.
Ritchie, G. *My Life After Dying: Becoming Alive to Universal Love*. Charlottesville, Va.: Hampton Roads Publishing, 1991.
Sabom, M. *Light and Death*. Grand Rapids, Mich.: Zondervan, 1998.
Valarino, E. *On the Other Side of Life*. New York: Plenum Press, 1997.
Woods, K. *Visions of the Bereaved: Hallucination or Reality?* Pittsburgh: Sterling House, 1998.
Zaleski, C. *Otherworld Journeys: Accounts of Near-Death Experience in Medieval and Modern Times*. New York: Oxford University Press, 1987.

Articles

Alvarado, C. "The Psychological Approach to Out-of-body Experiences: A Review of Early and Modern Developments." *Journal of Psychology* 126 (1992): 237–50.
Appleby, L. "Near-Death Experience: Analogous to Other Stress-induced Psychological Phenomena." *British Journal of Medicine* 298 (1989): 976–77.
Audette, J. R. "Historical Perspectives on Near-Death Experiences and Episodes." In *A Collection of Near-Death Readings*, edited by C. R. Lundahl. Chicago: Nelson Hall, 1982.
Barbato, M., C. Blunden, K. Reid, et al. "Parapsychological Phenomenon Near the Time of Death." *Journal of Palliative Care* 15, no. 2 (1999): 30–37.
Barrett, E. A. M., M. B. Doyle, V. M. Malinski, et al. "The Relationship Among the Experience of Dying, the Experience of Paranormal Events, and Creativity in Adults." In *Visions of Roger's Science-based Nursing*, edited by E. A. M. Barrett. New York: National League for Nursing Publication no. 15–2285, 1990.

Bates, B. C., and A. Stanley. "The Epidemiology and Differential Diagnosis of Near-Death Experience." *American Journal of Orthopsychiatry* 55 (1985): 542–49.

Becker, C. B. "The Pure Land Revisited: Sino-Japanese Meditations and Near-Death Experiences of the Next World." *Anabiosis: The Journal of Near-Death Studies* 4 (1984): 51–68.

Blackmore, S. "Out-of-body Experiences in Schizophrenia." *Journal of Nervous and Mental Disease* 174 (1986): 615–19.

———. "Visions from the Dying Brain." *New Scientist* (May 5, 1988): 43–46.

Burch, G. E., N. O. DePasquale, and J. H. Phillips. "What Death Is Like." *American Heart Journal* 76 (1968): 1438–39.

Carr, C. "Death and Near-death: A Comparison of Tibetan and Euro-American Experiences." *Journal of Transpersonal Psychology* 25 (1993): 59–110.

Comer, N. L., L. Madow, and J. J. Dixon. "Observations of Sensory Deprivation in a Life-threatening Situation." *American Journal of Psychiatry* 124 (1967): 164–70.

Druss, R. G., and D. S. Kornfield. "The Survivors of Cardiac Arrest: A Psychiatric Study." *Journal of the American Medical Association* 201 (1967): 291–96.

Greyson, B. "The Near-Death Experience Scale: Construction, Reliability and Validity." *Journal of Nervous and Mental Disease* 171 (1983): 369–75.

Greyson, B., and N. E. Bush. "Distressing Near-Death Experiences." *Psychiatry* 55 (1992): 95–110.

Greyson, B., and I. Stevenson. "Near-Death Experiences." *Journal of the American Medical Association* 242 (1979): 265–67.

———. "The Phenomenology of Near-Death Experiences." *American Journal of Psychiatry* 137 (1980): 1193–95.

Grimby, A. "Bereavement Among Elderly People: Grief Reactions, Postbereavement Hallucinations and Quality of Life." *Acta Psychiatric Scandinavia* 87 (1993): 72–80.

Gruen, A. "Relationship of Sudden Infant Death and Parental Unconscious Conflicts." *Pre- and Perinatal Psychology Journal* 2 (1982): 50–56.

Hackett, T. P. "The Lazarus Complex Revisted." *Annals of Internal Medicine* 76 (1972): 135–37.

Hallowell, I. "Spirits of the Dead in Saulteaux Life and Thought." *Journal of the Royal Anthropological Institute* 70 (1940): 29–51.

Haraldsson, E. "Survey of Claimed Encounters with the Dead." *Omega* 19 (1988–89): 103–13.

Heim, A. "Notizen über den Tod durch Absturz." *Jahrbuch des Schweizer Alpenclubs* 27 (1892): 327–37. Translated by R. Noyes and R. Kletti. "The Experience of Dying from Falls." *Omega* (1972): 45–52.

Hennsley, J. A., P. J. Christenson, R. A. Hardoin, et al. "Premonitions of Sudden Infant Death Syndrome: A Retrospective Case Control Study." Abstract of a paper presented at the National SIDS Alliance Meeting, Pittsburgh, October 1993. *Pediatric Pulmonology* 16 (1993): 393.

Hertzog, D. B., and J. T. Herrin. "Near-Death Experiences in the Very Young." *Critical Care Medicine* 13 (1985): 1074–75.

Hunter, R. C. A. "On the Experience of Nearly Dying." *American Journal of Psychiatry* 124 (1967): 122–23.

Jansen, K. R. "The Near-Death Experience." Letter in *Lancet* 153 (1988): 883–84.

Judson, I. R.A. and E. Wiltshaw. "A Near-Death Experience." *Lancet* 2 (1983): 561–62.

Kalish, R. A. "Experiences of Persons Reprieved from Death." In *Death and Bereavement*, edited by A. H. Kitscher. Springfield, Ill.: Charles C. Thomas, 1969.

Kalish, R. A., and D. K. Reynolds. "Phenomenological Reality and Post-death Contact." *Journal of Science and Study of Religion* (1973): 209–21.

Kross, J., and B. Bachrach. "Visions and Psychopathology in the Middle Ages." *Journal of Nervous and Mental Diseases* 170 (1982): 41–49.

Levin, C., and M. Curley. "Near-Death Experiences in Children." Paper presented at Perspective on Change: Forces Shaping Practice for the Clinical Nurse Specialist, Boston Children's Hospital, October 11, 1990.

MacMillan, R. L., and K. W. G. Brown. "Cardiac Arrest Remembered." *Canadian Medical Association Journal* 104 (1971): 889–90.

Matchett, W. F. "Repeated Hallucinatory Experiences as Part of the Mourning Process Among Hopi Indian Women." *Psychiatry* 35 (1972): 185–94.

Morse, M. L. "A Near-Death Experience in a 7-year-old Child." *American Journal of Diseases of Children* 137 (1983): 959–61.

Morse, M. L., P. Castillo, and D. Venecia. "Childhood Near-Death Experiences." *Am J Dis Child* 140 (1986): 110–14.

Morse, M. L., and V. M. Neppe. "Near-Death Experiences." Letter in *Lancet* 337 (1991): 386.

Negovsky, V. A. "Reanimatology Today." *Critical Care Medicine* 10 (1982): 130–33.

Noyes, R. "Near-Death Experiences: Their Interpretation and Significance." In *Between Life and Death*, by R. Kastenbaum. New York: Springer Publishing, 1979.

Noyes, R., P. R. Hoenk, S. Kuperman, et al. "Depersonalization in Accident Victims and Psychiatric Patients." *Journal of Nervous and Mental Disease* 164 (1977): 401–7.

Noyes, R., and R. Kletti. "Depersonalization in the Face of Life-threatening Danger: A Description." *Psychiatry* 39 (1976): 19–27.

Olson, M. "The Out-of-Body Experience and Other States of Consciousness." *Archives of Psychiatric Nursing* 1 (1987): 201–7.

Owens, J. E. E. W. Cook, and I. Stevenson. "Features of Near-Death Experience in Relation to Whether or Not Patients Were Near Death." *Lancet* 336 (1990): 1175–77.

Rees, W. D. "The Hallucinations of Widowhood." *British Journal of Medicine* 4 (1971): 37–41.

Roberts, G., and J. Owen. "The Near-Death Experience." *British Journal of Psychiatry* 153 (1988): 607–17.

Sabom, M. B., and S. A. Kreutiger. "Physicians Evaluate the Near-Death Experience." *Journal of the Florida Medical Association* 6 (1978): 1–6.

Schnaper, N. "The Psychological Implications of Severe Trauma: Emotional Sequelae to Unconsciousness." *J Trauma* 15 (1975): 94–98.

Schoonmaker, F. "Near-Death Experiences." *Anabiosis: The Journal of Near-Death Studies* 1 (1979): 1–35.

Schroeter-Kunhardt, M. "A Review of Near-Death Experiences." *Journal of Scientific Exploration* 7 (1993): 219–39.

————. "Erfahrungen sterbender während des klinischen Todes." *Zeitung Allgemeine Medizin* 66 (1990): 1014–21.

Serdahely, W. J. "Pediatric Death Experiences." *Journal of Near-Death Studies* 9 (1990): 33–41.

Sigel, R. K. "The Psychology of Life after Death." *American Psychology* 35 (1980): 911–31.

Tosch, P. "Patients' Recollections of Their Posttraumatic Coma." *Journal of Neuroscience and Nursing* 20 (1988): 223–28.

Vicchio, S. "Near-Death Experiences: A Critical Review of the Literature and Some Questions for Further Study." *Essence* 5 (1981): 79.

Walker, F. O. "A Nowhere Near Death Experience: Heavenly Choirs Interrupt Myelography." Letter in *Journal of the American Medical Association* 261 (1989): 1282–89.

Yates, T. T., and J. R. Bannard. "The Haunted Child: Grief, Hallucinations and Family Dynamics." *Journal of the American Academy of Child and Adolescent Psychiatry* 27 (1988): 673–91.

REFERENCES ON THE SCIENTIFIC STUDY
OF THE PARANORMAL

Books

Almeder, R. *Death and Personal Survival: The Evidence for Life After Death*. Lanham, Md.: Littlefield Adams Quality Paperbacks, 1992.

Auerbach, L. *ESP, Haunting and Poltergeists: A Parapsychologist's Handbook*. New York: Warner Books, 1986.

———. *Psychic Dreaming: A Parapsychologist's Handbook*. New York: Warner Books, 1991.

———. *Reincarnation, Channeling and Possession: A Parapsychologist's Handbook*. New York: Warner Books, 1993.

Blackmore, S. *Beyond the Body*. Chicago: Academy Chicago Publishers, 1992.

Broughton, R. *Parapsychology: The Controversial Science*. New York: Ballantine Books, 1991.

Duncan, L. *Who Killed My Daughter?* New York: Delacorte Press, 1992.

Duncan, L., and W. Roll. *Psychic Connections: A Journey into the Mysterious World of PSI*. New York: Delacorte Press, 1995.

Gabbard, G. O., and S. W. Twemlow. *With the Eyes of the Mind: An Empirical Analysis of Out-of-body States*. New York: Praeger, 1984.

Harpur, T. *Life After Death*. Toronto: McClelland and Stewart, 1991.

Hufford, D. *The Terror That Comes in the Night*. Philadelphia: University of Pennsylvania Press, 1982.

Jahn, R., and B. Dunne. *Margins of Reality: The Role of Consciousness in the Physical World*. San Diego: Harcourt Brace, 1987.

Koestler, A. *The Roots of Coincidence*. New York: Random House, 1972.

Myers, F. W. H. *Human Personality and Its Survival of Bodily Death*. 2 vols. New York: Longmans, Green and Co., 1903.

Mysteries of the Unknown: Phantom Encounters. Alexandria, Va.: Time-Life Books, 1988.

Mysteries of the Unknown: Spirit Summonings. Alexandria, Va.: Time-Life Books, 1989.

Ostrander, S., and L. Schroeder. *Psychic Discoveries Behind the Iron Curtain*. New York: Bantam Books, 1970.

Radin, D. *The Conscious Universe: The Scientific Truth of Psychic Phenomena*. New York: Harper Edge, 1997.

Schnabel, J. *Remote Viewers: The Secret History of America's Psychic Spies*. New York: Dell, 1997.

———. *Round in Circles: Poltergeists, Pranksters, and the Secret History of Cropwatchers*. New York: Prometheus Books, 1994.

Stapp, H. *Mind, Matter, and Quantum Mechanics.* New York: Springer-Verlag, 1993.

Talbot, M. *The Holographic Universe.* New York: HarperCollins, 1992.

Wilson I. *The After-Death Experience.* New York: Quill, 1987.

Articles

Barrett, E. A. M., M. B. Doyle, V. M. Malinski, et al. "The Relationship Among the Experience of Dying, the Experience of Paranormal Events, and Creativity in Adults." In *Visions of Roger's Science-based Nursing,* edited by E. A. M. Barrett. New York: National League for Nursing Publication no. 15-2285, 1990.

Bem, D., and C. Honorton. "Does PSI Exist? Replicable Evidence for an Anomalous Process of Information Transfer." *Psychological Bulletin* 115 (1994): 4-18.

Beutler, J., and J. Attevelt. "Paranormal Healing and Hypertension." *British Medical Journal* 296 (1988): 1491-94.

Braud, W., and S. Dennis. "Geophysical Variables and Behavior: Autonomic Activity Hemolysis, and Biological Psychokinesis: Possible Relationships with Geomagnetic Field Activity." *Perceptual and Motor Skills* 68 (1989): 1243-54.

Gruen, A. "Relationship of Sudden Infant Death and Parental Unconscious Conflicts." *Pre- and Perinatal Psychology Journal* 2 (1982): 50-56.

Haraldsson, E., and L. Gissurarson. "Does Geomagnetic Activity Affect Extrasensory Perception?" *Personality and Individual Differences* 8 (1987): 745-47.

Hennsley, J. A., P. J. Christenson, R. A. Hardoin, et al. "Premonitions of Sudden Infant Death Syndrome: A Retrospective Case Control Study. Abstract of paper presented at the National SIDS Alliance Meeting, Pittsburgh, October 1993. *Pediatric Pulmonology* 16 (1993): 393.

Hufford, J. D. "Paranormal Experiences in the General Population: A Commentary." *Journal of Nervous and Mental Disease* 180 (1992): 362-68.

Hyman, R. "Parapsychological Research: Tutorial Review and Critical Appraisal." *Proceedings of the IEEE* 74 (1985): 823-49.

Jahn, R. "The Persistent Paradox of Psychic Phenomena: Engineering Perspective." *Proceedings of the IEEE* 70 (1982): 136-70.

Kohr, R. L. "Near-Death Experiences, Altered States and PSI Sensitivity." *Anabiosis: The Journal of Near-Death Studies* 3 (1983): 157-76.

Kuang, K. "Long-term Observation on QiGong in Prevention of Stroke: Follow-up 244 Hypertensive Patients for 18–22 Years." *Journal of Traditional Chinese Medicine* 6, no. 4 (1986): 235–38.

Milne, G. "Hypnotherapy with Migraine." *Australian Journal of Clinical and Experimental Hypnosis* 2, no. 3 (1982): 23–32.

Nelson, G. K. "Preliminary Study of the EEG of Mediums." *Parapsychologica* 4 (1970): 30–45.

Neppe, V. M. "PSI, Genetics, and the Temporal Lobes." *Parapsychological Journal of South Africa*, 2, no. 1 (1981): 35–55.

———. "The Temporal Lobe and Anomalous Experience." *Parapsychological Journal of South Africa* 5, no. 1 (1984): 36–47.

Penfield, W. "The Role of the Temporal Cortex in Certain Psychical Phenomena." *Journal of Mental Science* 101 (1955): 451–65.

Rao, K., and J. Palmer. "The Anomaly Called PSI: Recent Research and Criticism." *Behavioral and Brain Sciences* 10 (1987): 539–51.

Stapp, H. "Theoretical Model of a Purported Empirical Violation of the Predictions of Quantum Theory." *Physical Review* 50 (1994): 18 22.

Tobacyk, J. "Death Threat, Death Concerns, and Paranormal Belief." *Death Education* 7 (1983): 115–24.

Utts, J. "An Assessment of the Evidence for Psychic Functioning." *Journal of Scientific Exploration* 10 (1999): 3–30.

REFERENCES FOR SCIENTIFIC PERSPECTIVE ON RELIGION, SPIRITUALITY, AND CONSCIOUSNESS

Books

Calvin, W. *The Cerebral Symphony.* New York: Bantam Books, 1989.

Capra, F. *The Tao of Physics.* New York: Bantam Books, 1976.

Crick, F. *The Astonishing Hypothesis: The Scientific Search for the Soul.* New York: Charles Scribner's Sons, 1994.

Davies, P. *The Mind of God: The Scientific Basis for a Rational World.* New York: Touchstone, 1992.

Dennett, D. *Consciousness Explained.* Boston: Little, Brown, 1991.

Dossey, L. *Recovering the Soul: A Scientific and Spiritual Search.* New York: Bantam Books, 1989.

Ferris, T. *The Mind's Sky: Human Intelligence in a Cosmic Context.* New York: Bantam Books, 1992.

Gerber, R. *Vibrational Medicine.* Santa Fe: Bear and Co., 1988.

Gibson, A. *Fingerprints of God.* Bountiful, Utah: Horizon Publishers, 1999.

Grof, S. *The Holotropic Mind.* San Francisco: HarperSan Francisco, 1990.

Hofstadter, D., and D. Dennett. *The Mind's I: Fantasies and Reflections on Self and Soul.* New York: Bantam Books, 1981.

Huxley, A. *The Doors of Perception / Heaven and Hell.* New York: HarperPerennial, 1990.

Lederman, L., and D. Teresi. *The God Particle: If the Universe Is the Answer, What Is the Question?* New York: Delta, 1993.

Lewels, J. *The God Hypothesis.* Mill Spring, N.C.: Wild Flower Press, 1997.

Lorimer, D., ed. *The Spirit of Science: From Experiment to Experience.* Harrison Gardens, Edinburgh: Floris Books, 1998.

Maslow, A. H. *The Farther Reaches of Human Nature.* New York: Viking Press, 1971.

Peat, F. *Synchronicity: The Bridge Between Matter and Mind.* New York: Bantam Books, 1987.

Penfield, W. *The Mystery of the Mind.* Princeton, N.J.: Princeton University Press, 1975.

Restak, R. *The Brain Has a Mind of Its Own.* New York: Harmony Books, 1991.

Richards, P. S., and A. E. Bergin. *A Spiritual Strategy for Counseling and Psychotherapy.* Washington, D.C.: American Psychological Association, 1997.

Sagan, C. *The Demon-Haunted World: Science as a Candle in the Dark.* New York: Ballantine Books, 1996.

Schrödinger, E. *What Is Life?* New York: Cambridge University Press, 1992.

Schroeder, G. *The Science of God: The Convergence of Scientific and Biblical Wisdom.* New York: The Free Press, 1997.

Searle, J. *Minds, Brains and Science.* Cambridge, Mass.: Harvard University Press, 1984.

Tart, C. *Body Mind Spirit.* Charlottesville, Va.: Hampton Roads Publishing, 1997.

Tiller, W. *Science and Human Transformation: Subtle Energies, Intentionality and Consciousness.* Walnut Creek, Calif.: Pavior, 1997.

Tipler, F. *The Physics of Immortality.* New York: Anchor Books, 1994.

Young, J. *Philosophy and the Brain.* New York: Oxford University Press, 1988.

Zukav, G. *The Dancing Wu Li Masters.* New York: William Morrow, 1980.

———. *The Seat of the Soul.* New York: Fireside, 1989.

Articles

Boutell, K. A., and B. W. Frederick. "Nurses' Assessment of Patients' Spirituality: Continuing Education Implications." *Journal of Continuing Education in Nursing* 21, no. 4 (1992): 172–76.

Burkhardt, M. "Spirituality: An Analysis of the Concept." *Holistic Nursing Practice* (May 1989): 60–77.

Cawley, N. "An Exploration of the Concept of Spirituality." *International Journal of Palliative Nursing* 3, no. 1 (1997): 31–36.

Dudley, J. R., C. Smith, and M. B. Millison. "Unfinished Business: Assessing the Spiritual Needs of Hospice Clients." *American Journal of Hospice and Palliative Care* (March–April 1995): 30–37.

Engebretson, J. "Considerations in Diagnosing in the Spiritual Domain." *Nursing Diagnosis* 7, no. 3 (July–September 1996): 100–107.

Florell, J. L. "Crisis Intervention in Orthopedic Surgery: Empirical Evidence of the Effectiveness of a Chaplain Working with Surgery Patients." *Bulletin of the American Protestant Hospital Association* 37 (1973): 29–36.

Gardner, R. "Miracles of Healing in Anglo-Celtic Northumbria as Recorded by the Venerable Bede and His Contemporaries: A Reappraisal in the Light of the Twentieth-century Experience." *British Journal of Medicine* 287 (1983): 24–31.

Guy, R. F. "Religion, Physical Disabilities, and Life Satisfaction in Older Age Cohorts." *International Journal of Aging and Human Development* 15 (1982): 225–32.

Hay, M. W. "Principles in Building Spiritual Assessment Tools." *Am J Hospice Care* (September–October 1989): 25–31.

Heliker, D. "Reevaluation of a Nursing Diagnosis: Spiritual Distress." *Nursing Forum* 27, no. 4 (October–December 1992): 15–20.

Highfield, M. F., and C. Carson. "The Spiritual Needs of Patients: Are They Recognized?" *Cancer Nursing* 6 (1983): 187.

MacDonald, S. M., R. Sandmaier, and R. L. Fainsinger. "Objective Evaluation of Spiritual Care: A Case Report." *Journal of Palliative Care* 9, no. 2 (1993): 47–49.

Mandell, A. "Toward a Psychobiology of Transcendence: God in the Brain." In *The Psychobiology of Consciousness*, edited by R.S. Davidson. New York: Plenum Press, 1980.

Mansen, T. J. "The Spiritual Dimension of Individuals: Conceptual Development." *Nursing Diagnosis* 4, no. 4 (October–December 1993): 140–47.

McSherry, E., D. Kratz, and W. A. Nelson. "Pastoral Care Departments: More Necessary in the DRG Era." *Health Care Management Review* 11 (1986): 47–61.

Merman, A. C. "Spiritual Aspects of Death and Dying." *Yale Journal of Biology and Medicine* 65 (1992): 137–42.

Millison, M. B. "A Review of the Research on Spiritual Care and Hospice." *The Hospice Journal* 10, no. 4 (1995): 3–18.

O'Connor, P. "The Role of Spiritual Care in Hospice." *American Journal of Hospice Care* 5, no. 4 (1988): 31–37.

———. "Spiritual Care Meets Palliative Care." *Vision* (May 1999): 9–10.

Persinger, M. "Religious and Mystical Experience as Artifacts of Temporal Lobe Function: A General Hypothesis." *Perceptual and Motor Skills* 57 (1983): 1255–62.

Reed, P. G. "An Emerging Paradigm for the Investigation of Spirituality in Nursing. *Research in Nursing and Health* 15 (1992): 349–57.

———. "Spirituality and Well-Being in Terminally Ill Hospitalized Patients." *Research in Nursing and Health* 10 (1987): 335–44.

Sodestrum, K. E., and I. M. Martinson. "Patients' Spiritual Coping." *Strategies: A Study of Nurse and Patient Perspective* 14, no. 2 (1987): 41–46.

Speck, P. W. "Spiritual Issues in Palliative Care." In *Oxford Textbook of Palliative Medicine*, edited by D. Doyle, G. W. C. Hanks, and N. MacDonald. Oxford: Oxford University Press, 1993.

Stoll, R. I. "Guidelines for Spiritual Assessment." *AJN* (September 1979): 1574–75.

Sumner, C. H. "Recognizing and Responding to Spiritual Needs." *American Journal of Nursing* 98, no. 1 (1998): 26–30.

VandeCreek, L., S. Ayres, and M. Bassham. "Using INSPIRIT to Conduct Spiritual Assessments." *Journal of Pastoral Care* 49, no. 4 (Spring 1995): 83–90.

REFERENCES ON MIND-BODY HEALING

Books

Benson, H. *Beyond the Relaxation Response.* New York: Berkley Publishing Group, 1984.

Benson, H., and E. Stuart. *The Wellness Book: The Comprehensive Guide to Maintaining Health and Treating Stress-Related Illness.* New York: Fireside, 1992.

Bessett, L., ed. *Beyond Suffering or Death.* Quebec: MNH, 1994.

Chopra, D. *Quantum Healing: Exploring the Frontiers of mind-body Medicine.* New York: Bantam Books, 1989.

Cornwell, J. *The Hiding Places of God.* New York: Warner, 1991.

Cousins, N. *Head First: The Biology of Hope and the Healing Power of the Human Spirit.* New York: Penguin, 1989.

Cranston, R. *The Miracle of Lourdes.* New York: Doubleday, 1988.

Dethlefsen, T., and R. Dahlke. *The Healing Power of Illness: The Meaning of Symptoms and How to Interpret Them.* Rockport, Mass.: Element Books, 1990.

Dossey, L. *Meaning and Medicine: A Doctor's Tales of Breakthrough and Healing.* New York: Bantam Books, 1991.

———. *Space, Time and Medicine.* Boston: Shambhala, 1982.

Glasser, W. *Stations of the Mind: New Directions for Reality Therapy.* New York: Harper and Row, 1981.

Goleman, D., and J. Gurin, eds. *Mind-Body Medicine: How to Use Your Mind for Better Health.* Yonkers, N.Y.: Consumer Reports Books, 1993.

Hirshberg, C., and M. Barasch. *Remarkable Recovery: What Extraordinary Healings Tell Us About Getting Well and Staying Well.* New York: Riverhead Books, 1995.

Hutchison, M. *The Book of Floating: Exploring the Private Sea.* New York: Quill, 1982.

Kharitidi, O. *Entering the Circle: Ancient Secrets of Siberian Wisdom Discovered by a Russian Psychiatrist.* San Francisco: Harper San Francisco, 1996.

Kunz, D. *Spiritual Aspects of the Healing Arts.* Wheaton, Ill.: Quest Books, 1985.

LeShan, L. *The Medium, the Mystic, and the Physicist.* New York: Viking, 1974.

Liu, H., and P. Perry. *Mastering Miracles: The Healing Art of Qi Gong as Taught by a Master.* New York: Warner, 1997.

Moyers, B. *Healing and the Mind.* New York: Doubleday, 1993.

Myss, C. *Anatomy of the Spirit: The Seven Stages of Power and Healing.* New York: Three Rivers Press, 1996.

———. *Why People Don't Heal and How They Can.* New York: Harmony Books, 1997.

Pearsall, P. *Making Miracles: Finding Meaning in Life's Chaos.* New York: Avon, 1991.

Plotkin, M. *Tales of a Shaman's Apprentice.* New York: Penguin, 1994.

Porter, G., and P. Norris. *Why Me? Harnessing the Healing Power of the Human Spirit.* Walpole, N.H.: Stillpoint Publishing, 1985.

Sheikh, A., ed. *Imagination and Healing.* Imagery and Human Development Series. Farmingdale, N.Y.: Baywood Publishing, 1984.

Targ, R., and J. Katra. *Miracles of Mind: Exploring Nonlocal Consciousness and Spiritual Healing.* Novato, Calif.: New World Library, 1998.

Weiss, B. *Through Time into Healing: Discovering the Power of Regression Therapy to Erase Trauma and Transform Mind, Body, and Relationships.* New York: Fireside, 1992.

White, L., B. Tursky, and G. Schwartz. *Placebo: Theory, Research and Mechanics.* New York: Guilford Press, 1985.

Articles

Ader, R., and N. Cohen. "Behaviorally Conditioned Immunosupression." *Psychosomatic Medicine* 37, no. 4 (1975): 333–40.

Baker, H. "Spontaneous Regression of Malignant Melanoma." *American Surgeon* 30, no. 12 (1964): 825–29.

Barber, T. "Changing Unchangeable Processes by Hypnotic Suggestion: A New Look at Hypnosis, Cognition, Imagining and the Mind-Body Problem." *Advances* 1, no. 2 (1984): 30–34.

Bell, J., J. Jesseph, and R. Leighton. "Spontaneous Regression of Bronchogenic Carcinoma with Five-year Survival." *Journal of Thoracic and Cardiovascular Surgery* 48, no. 6 (1964): 984–90.

Clawson, T., and R. Swade. "The Hypnotic Control of Blood Flow and Pain: The Cure of Warts and the Potential of the Use of Hypnosis in the Treatment of Cancer." *American Journal of Clinical Hypnosis* 17 (1975): 160–69.

Goodwin, J. "The Effect of Marital Status on Stage, Treatment and Survival of Cancer Patients." *Journal of the American Medical Association* 258, no. 21 (1987): 3125.

Greenleaf, M. "Hypnotizability and Recovery from Cardiac Surgery." *American Journal of Clincal Hypnosis* 35, no. 2 (1992): 119–29.

Grillet, B., M. Demedts, and J. Roelens. "Spontaneous Regression of Lung Metasteses of Adenocystic Carcinoma." *Chest* 85, no. 2 (1984): 289–91.

Hall, H. "Hypnosis and the Immune System: A Review with Implications for Cancer and the Psychology of Healing." *American Journal of Clinical Hypnosis* 25, nos. 2–3 (1982–1983).

Ikemi, Y. "Psychosomatic Consideration on Cancer Patients Who Have Made a Narrow Escape from Death." *Dynamic Psychiatry* 8, no. 2 (1975): 85.

Kanigel, R. "Placebos: Magic Medicine?" *Johns Hopkins Magazine* (August 1983): 12–16.

Kennedy, S., J. Keicolt-Glasser, and R. Glasser. "Immunological Consequences of Acute and Chronic Stressors in a Mediating Role of Interpersonal Relationships." *British Journal of Medical Psychology* 61 (1988): 77–85.

Klopfer, B. "Psychological Variables in Human Cancer." *Journal of Projective Techniques* 21 (1957): 329–40.

Lam, K., J. Ho, and R. Yeung. "Spontaneous Regression of Hepatocellular Carcinoma: A Case Study." *Cancer* 50, no. 2 (1982): 332–36.

LeShan, L., and M. Gassman. "Some Observations on Psychotherapy on Patients with Neoplastic Disease." *American Journal of Psychotherapy* 12 (1958): 723–34.

O'Regan, B., and T. Hurley. "Placebo: The Hidden Asset in Healing." *Investigations* (Research Bulletin of the Institute of Noetic Sciences) 2, no. 1 (1985): 5.

Peschel, R., and E. Peschel. "Medical Miracles from the Physician-Scientist Point of View." *Perspectives in Biology and Medicine* 31, no. 3 (1988): 392.

Shen, G. "The Study of Mind-Body Effects and Qi Gong in China." *Advances* 3, no. 4 (1986): 139–40.

Sinclair-Gieben, A., and D. Chalmers. "Evaluation of Treatment of Warts by Hypnosis." *Lancet* 2 (1959): 480–82.

Spiegel, D. "A Psychosocial Intervention in Survival Time of Patients with Metastatic Breast Cancer." *Advances* 7, no. 3 (1991): 15.

Stampley, E. "The Healing Power of Suggestion." *Tourovues* (1989): 1.

REFERENCES ON MEMORY AND PAST-LIFE MEMORIES

Books

Bowman, C. *Children's Past Lives: How Past Life Memories Affect Your Child.* New York: Bantam Books, 1997.

Chamberlain, D. *Babies Remember Birth.* Los Angeles: Jeremy P. Tarcher, 1988.

Ducasse, C. J. *A Critical Examination of the Belief in a Life After Death.* Springfield, Ill.: Charles C. Thomas, 1961.

Hallett, E. *Soul Trek: Meeting Our Children on the Way to Birth.* Hamilton, Mont.: Light Hearts Publishing, 1995.

Hinze, S. *Coming from the Light: Spiritual Accounts of Life Before Life.* New York: Pocket Books, 1997.

Loftus, E., and K. Ketcham. *Witness for the Defense.* New York: St. Martin's Press, 1991.

Lucas, W., ed. *Regression Therapy: A Handbook for Professionals.* 2 vols. Crest Park, Calif.: Deep Forest Press, 1993.

Rogo, D. S. *The Search for Yesterday: A Critical Examination of the Evidence for Reincarnation.* Englewood Cliffs, N.J.: Prentice-Hall, 1985.

Stevenson, I. *Cases of the Reincarnation Type.* Vol. 1: *Ten Cases in India.* Charlottesville, Va.: University Press of Virginia, 1975.

————. *Cases of the Reincarnation Type*. Vol. 3: *Twelve Cases in Lebanon and Turkey*. Charlottesville, Va.: University Press of Virginia, 1980.

————. *Children Who Remember Previous Lives*. Charlottesville, Va.: University Press of Virginia, 1987.

————. *Twenty Cases Suggestive of Reincarnation*. Charlottesville, Va.: University Press of Virginia, 1974.

Terr, L. *Unchained Memories: True Stories of Traumatic Memories Lost and Found*. New York: Basic Books, 1994.

Articles

Stevenson, I. "American Children Who Claim to Remember Previous Lives." *Journal of Nervous and Mental Disease* 171, no. 12 (1983): 742–48.

————. "Birthmarks and Birth Defects Corresponding to Wounds on Deceased Persons." *Journal of Scientific Exploration* 7, no. 4 (1993): 403–10.

————. "Phobias in Children Who Claim to Remember Previous Lives." *Journal of Scientific Exploration* 4, no. 2 (1990): 243–54.

REFERENCES ON RELIGION AND SPIRITUALITY

Books

Bragdon, E. *The Call of Spiritual Emergency*. San Francisco: Harper and Row, 1990.

Cowan, T. *Shamanism as a Spiritual Practice for Daily Life*. Freedom, Calif.: The Crossing Press, 1996.

Eliade, M. *Shamanism: Archaic Techniques of Ecstasy*. Princeton: Princeton University Press, 1964.

Evans-Wentz, W. *The Tibetan Book of the Dead*. London: Oxford University Press, 1960.

Flanagan, S. *Secrets of God: Writings of Hildegard of Bingen*. Boston: Shambhala, 1996.

Frazer, J. *The New Golden Bough*. New York: New American Library, 1959.

Harner, M. *The Way of the Shaman*. San Francisco: HarperSan Francisco, 1990.

Hauck, R., ed. *Angels: The Mysterious Messengers*. New York: Ballantine Books, 1994.

Hick, J. *An Interpretation of Religion: Human Responses to the Transcendent*. New Haven: Yale University Press, 1989.

Ingersoll, R. *Reason, Tolerance, and Christianity: The Ingersoll Debates*. New York: Prometheus Books, 1993.

James, W. *The Varieties of Religious Experience*. New York: The Modern
Library, 1902.

Keller, H. *Light in My Darkness*. West Chester, Penn.: Chrysalis Books,
1994.

Moore, T. *Care of the Soul: A Guide for Cultivating Depth and Sacred-
ness in Everyday Life*. New York: HarperPerennial, 1992.

Moss, R. *Conscious Dreaming*. New York: Three Rivers Press, 1996.

Rampa, T. *The Third Eye*. New York: Ballantine Books, 1995.

Rinpoche, S. *The Tibetan Book of Living and Dying*. San Francisco:
Harper San Francisco, 1992.

Schucman, H., and W. Thetford. *A Course in Miracles*. New York: Penguin, 1996.

MISCELLANEOUS REFERENCES

Books

Becker, G. de. *The Gift of Fear: Survival Signals That Protect Us from Violence*. New York: Little, Brown, 1997.

Campbell, J. *Creative Mythology: The Masks of God*. New York: Penguin, 1968.

————. *Myths to Live by*. New York: Bantam Books, 1972.

————. *The Power of Myth*. New York: Doubleday, 1984.

————. *Primitive Mythology*. New York: Penguin, 1967.

Davis, W. *Shadows in the Sun: Travel to Landscapes of Spirit and Desire*.
Washington, D.C.: Island Press, 1998.

Eliach, Y. *Hasidic Tales of the Holocaust*. New York: Vintage, 1988.

Furst, P. *Hallucinogens and Culture*. San Francisco: Chandler and Sharp,
1976.

Hall, E. *The Hidden Dimension*. New York: Anchor Books, 1982.

Jovanovic, P. *An Inquiry into the Existence of Guardian Angels*. New
York: M. Evans and Co., 1993.

Meltzer, D. *Death: An Anthology of Ancient Texts, Songs, Prayers, and
Stories*. San Francisco: North Point Press, 1984.

Miles, M. B., and A. M. Huberman. *Qualitative Data Analysis: A
Sourcebook of New Methods*. Newbury Park, Calif.: Sage Publications,
1984.

Monroe, R. *Journeys out of the Body*. New York: Doubleday, 1977.

Norman, M., and B. Scott. *Historic Haunted America*. New York: A Tom
Doherty Associates Book, 1995.

Nuland, S. *How We Die: Reflections on Life's Final Chapter*. New York:
Alfred A. Knopf, 1994.

Pearce, C. S. *A Crack in the Cosmic Egg*. New York: Pocket Books, 1971.
Popescu, P. *Amazon Beaming*. New York: Viking, 1991.
Ring, K. *Near-Death Experiences: UFOs and Mind at Large*. New York: Macmillan, 1992.
Rothenberg, J. *Technicians of the Sacred*. New York: Anchor Books, 1968.
Sacks, O. *An Anthropologist on Mars: Seven Paradoxical Tales*. New York: Alfred A. Knopf, 1995.
Sagan, C. *Broca's Brain*. New York: Random House, 1979.
Thompson, C. *The Mystery and Lore of Apparitions*. Detroit: Gale Research Co., 1974.
Thompson, K. *Angels and Aliens*. New York: Fawcett Columbine, 1991.
Vandereycken, W., and R. van Deth. *From Fasting Saints to Anorexic Girls: The History of Self-Starvation*. New York: New York University Press, 1994.

Articles

Hansen, G. P. "CSICOP and the Skeptics: An Overview." *Journal of American Society for Psychical Research* 86, no. 1 (1992): 19–63.
Holman, H. R. "Qualitative Inquiry in Medical Research." *Journal of Clinical Epidemiology* 46 (1993): 29–36.
Kirschvink, Kobayashi-Kirschvink, and Woolford. "Magnetic Biomineralization in the Human Brain." *Proceedings of the National Academy of Science* 89 (1992): 7683–87.
Stevenson, I. "Do We Need a New Word to Supplement 'Hallucination?'" *Am I Psychiatry* 140 (1983): 1609–11.

Journals

Advances: The Journal of Mind-Body Health. Published by the John Fetzer Institute, 9292 West KL Avenue, Kalamazoo, MI 49009-9398. This journal contains well-referenced scientific articles on consciousness and mind-body healing, written by top scientists and physicians.
Exceptional Human Experience. Published by Rhea White, The Exceptional Human Experience Network, New Bern, NC 28562. Rhea White is a prominent parapsychological researcher who now publishes anecdotal experiences and articles on the entire range of different states of human consciousness.
Frontier Perspectives. Published by the Center for Frontier Sciences at Temple University, Temple University, Ritter Hall 003–00, Philadelphia, PA 19122. Written by scientists for scientists, this journal tackles cutting-edge issues and has been savaged by the *Skeptical Inquirer*. Nevertheless, it is the only journal I know of that presents

peer-reviewed, well-referenced scientific articles on issues currently way outside the realm of mainstream science.

Journal of Consciousness Studies: Controversies in Science and the Humanities. Published by Imprint Academics, Consciousness Studies, Department of Psychology, University of Arizona, 1433 E. Helen, Tucson, AZ 85721. This is a thick, densely written journal for scientists examining consciousness issues from a multidisciplinary point of view, including artists, neurobiologists, theologians, psychologists, philosophers, physicians, and biologists.

Journal of Irreproducible Results: The Official Organ of the Society for Basic Irreproducible Research. Published by George Scherr, Box 234, Chicago Heights, IL 60411. Featuring articles on "diet and the expanding universe," "precognitive transpersonal diagnosis and treatment," and "aggregate intelligence and the collective clown problem," this journal is a welcome reminder to have a good laugh every once in a while.

Journal of Near-Death Studies. Published by the Human Sciences Press, 233 Spring Street, New York, NY 10013–1578. Edited by Bruce Greyson, this journal publishes peer-reviewed scientific articles on near death experiences and related scientific fields.

Journal of Scientific Exploration. The journal of the Society for Scientific Exploration, P.O. Box 5848, Stanford, CA 94309. This journal is for unbiased mainstream scientists dedicated to the research and discussion of anomalous phenomena that lie outside the conventional disciplines of science, such as UFOs, the "face" on Mars, and consciousness research. Well referenced, written for scientists.

Network: The Scientific and Medical Network Review. Edited by David Lorimer, Gibliston Mill, Colinsburgh, Leven, Fife, KY9 1JS Scotland. This journal publishes well-referenced articles written by and for mainstream scientists and physicians who have an interest in new scientific paradigms. Their mission is to "deepen understanding in science, medicine and education by fostering both rational and intuitive insights."

Omega: The Journal of Death and Dying. Edited by Robert Kastenbaum, Baywood Publishing, P.O. Box 337, Amityville, NY 11701. This academic social science journal is dedicated to studying death and dying issues.

Parabola: Myth, Tradition, and the Search for Meaning. Quarterly publication of the Society for the Study of Myth and Tradition, P.O. Box 3000, Denville, NJ 07834. Each issue is devoted to presenting stories and myths from diverse cultures on a given topic, such as fear, death, or sin.

Skeptical Inquirer: The Magazine for Science and Reason. Published by the Committee for the Scientific Investigation of Claims of the Paranormal (CSICOPS), 1310 Sweet Home Road, Amherst NY 14228. This journal features well-referenced articles written for the general public. CSICOPS is a large, mainstream scientific organization dedicated to debunking everything from paranormal abilities to New Age con artists and alternative medicine.